How To

Survive

The Fringe

For Pam

The Perfect
Fringe Companion

Contents

Introduction

My first visit to the Edinburgh Fringe was some time in the early eighties. I was in town on business for a few days and some friends got me tickets for a couple of shows. To this day, I cannot remember what I saw or where, but I do remember that the ticket was a two inch square with blue borders and cost £2.50. Unlike these days where the tickets are printed on demand, at that time all the tickets were pre-printed in little books, just like raffle tickets. It is hard to see how the Fringe would cope if they had to use the same system today.

Looking back I think that, at least initially, it must have been the "value for money" aspect of the shows that impressed me, rather than the quality of the shows. Whatever it was, I continued to see a few shows each year on the same basis, but at some time I must have made a decision to visit Edinburgh and "do the Fringe" properly. Since 1991, I have visited the Fringe every year and have now seen over 400 shows.

The purpose of this publication is to give newcomers to the Fringe an insight into what to expect and how to make the most of the time spent in Edinburgh. By this I mean those who sit facing the stage. I am sure there is (or if there isn't, there should be) an equivalent book for those who perform at the Fringe but that is outside my area of expertise. I also hope that experienced Fringe attendees will enjoy the book by comparing my experiences with their own. They may even learn something useful.

It can by definition only be a personal view since there are so many aspects to the Fringe and each person will make the most of it in their own way. Another important point is that the Fringe evolves and every year there are changes. Venues, ticketing arrangements, programme details, dates, events, etc., can all vary from year to year so please check the situation for yourself. The information detailed in the following pages was produced after the 2007 Fringe.

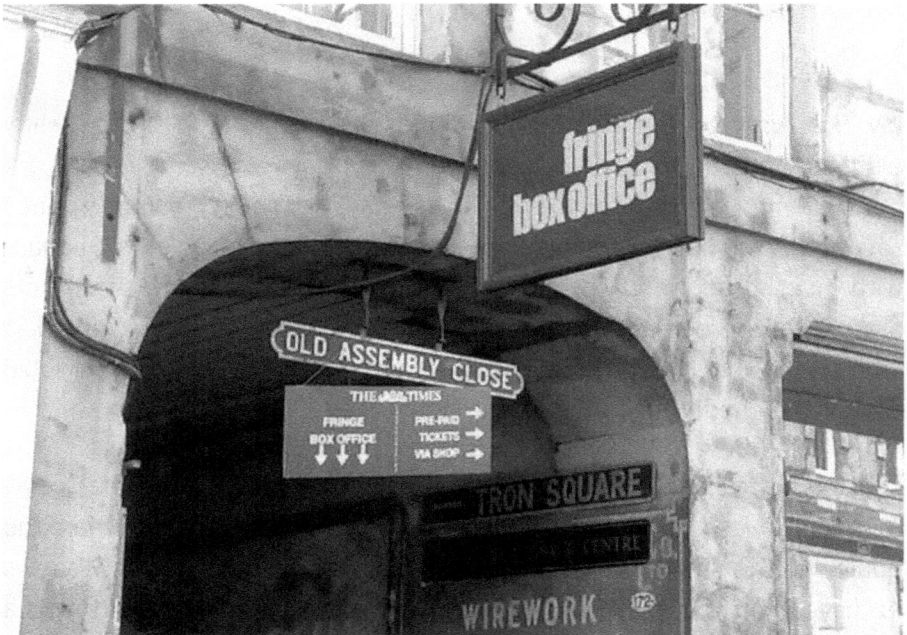
Alley leading to Fringe Box Office

Also, this book does not include a general guide to Edinburgh so there is no specific mention of Hotels and Restaurants. This sort of information is readily available in dozens of publications and on the Web. Also, there is no map of Edinburgh. The Fringe programme has a detailed map of the city showing the sites of the various Venues.

Although there are many other festivals going on in Edinburgh at the same time, I am going to concentrate on the Fringe Festival. Apart from a couple of forays into the International Festival and one trip to the

Tattoo, I have not visited these other events and many of the principles and advice I can offer do not really apply to them.

Some of the other festivals that are on around the same time as the Fringe are:

Jazz and Blues Festival (End July-Beginning August)

International Book Festival (Last two weeks August)

International Film Festival (Last two weeks August)

Military Tattoo (Same dates as the Fringe)

Mela (First weekend in September)

Television Festival (Bank Holiday Weekend)

If you want to see the Tattoo, book well in advance. By the time August arrives, all the tickets will be sold.

At the time of writing, there is a plan that the Film Festival is going to be moved to June.

Lastly, I may resort to the phrase "I seem to remember" more times than I should. It's just that at my time of life, the memory is not as good as it should be and I may have got things wrong. That's another good reason to check the information for yourself.

What Is It

It does seem a bit strange to me, someone who has visited the Fringe so many times, that the first thing I should perhaps do is to explain what the Fringe is. Looking back to the time before I first attended the Fringe, I can recall having an impression that it was some sort of intellectual get together and that it would not hold any attraction for me. As it turned out, that was far from the truth. In particular, I have in my mind a picture of Ned Sherrin reviewing very serious work on a late night BBC2 programme. Perhaps he was referring to the International Festival rather that the Fringe, I cannot remember now.

So what is the "Fringe"?

Well, the main Edinburgh International Festival (EIF) was started 1947. Its brief was to put on a mixture of classical music, opera, ballet, dance and serious theatre by companies from around the world. These were performed in a variety of Venues in Edinburgh but it was not until 1999 that the EIF gained its first permanent site, the Hub. It is at the top of the Royal Mile, near the Castle and this is where you can buy tickets for the EIF. It provides a central base for the EIF, but it is open all year round, providing a focal point for the culture of the city.

Such was the success of the EIF in the first year that eight theatre companies (six Scottish and two English) turned up uninvited to put on shows that were not part of the EIF, i.e. they were on the fringe of the main event. This process was repeated in subsequent years until, nearly 60 years later, the Edinburgh Festival Fringe now dwarfs the EIF, certainly in terms of ticket sales, if not artistically. Indeed, in recent years, the Fringe decided to change the dates during which it is held so that it no longer coincides exactly with the EIF. This was greeted with some protests at the time but in practice it does not appear to have made any difference overall. In fact, by spreading the two events over a longer period, there may be less strain on the facilities in the city, i.e. hotels and restaurants.

Royal Mile near Fringe Box Office

So the Fringe is an offshoot of the EIF, but what does it offer these days?

Well most people's reaction when I say that I go to the Fringe is to assume that I spend most of my time watching stand-up comedians. This impression comes from the fact that comedians receive most of the publicity. Indeed, it is hard to think of any current popular British comedians who have not appeared on the Fringe at some stage. There are many who appear on the Fringe every year and presumably they will continue to do so until they get their big break on television.

If I look through all the ticket stubs I have kept from past shows (yes, I am a sad person), they read like a Who's Who of British comedy. There's Eddie Izzard, Jack Dee, Steve Coogan, Harry Hill, Frank Skinner and many more. It's interesting to see how we rated them at the time (see chapter "Good, Bad and Ugly").

As a result stand-up comedy is the headline type of act, but in terms of the total number of shows they are in the minority. Looking at the shows I have seen over the years since 1991, over 200 were drama and less than 100 were stand-up comedians. The rest were a mixture of music, dance, circus, variety and the occasional children's show. Of the shows listed in the Fringe 2007 programme, 31% was Theatre and 30.5% was comedy. The rest was made up of Music (17%), Children's shows (5.5%), Musicals and Opera (5%), Dance and Physical Theatre (4.5%). The balance was Exhibitions and Events. The Comedy section has 86 pages but these are not just stand-up comedy shows, they also include other types of comedy. A quick scan of the shows seems to indicate that only a quarter at most are what you could broadly call "stand-up". Another quarter is comedy sketch shows and the rest drama. That means of the 2,000 shows in 2007, about 150 were stand-up comedy.

Of the 31 shows I saw in 2006, only 4 were stand-up comedians. In 2007, the figures were 7 out of 32 shows. So please do not think that the Fringe is just about stand-up comedy.

The Fringe is organised centrally by the Fringe Office, which has existed since 1958. It is based on the Royal Mile. Before it came into existence, tickets were sold for the various Fringe shows on an uncoordinated basis. The formation of the Fringe Office meant that you could go to one central point for tickets to all the shows. That is still true today, but be aware that sometimes the Fringe Office does not have tickets for popular shows because they have been withdrawn by the Venue. They may still be available directly from the Venue (See chapter 'How To Book').

The shows themselves are performed at various "Venues" around the city. These are given a unique Venue Number by the Fringe Office so that can be easily identified. Some consist of one stage and one show, while others have multiple stages and dozens of shows. They can be in pubs, bars, private houses and even caves. Sometimes there are outdoor Venues, e.g. the Botanical Gardens, and often the most atmospheric Venues are the disused churches.

The Venue buildings can be permanent performance spaces (e.g. The Traverse) but most often they are used only during the Fringe (e.g. The Gilded Balloon, which uses the University buildings near Bristo Square). It is probably fair to say that there is no space too small for a Fringe show. If you doubt this, bear in mind that there have been shows performed in a moving car.

When referring to "Venues", I will try to be consistent in my references as follows:

A Venue is the umbrella organisation, e.g. The Assembly Rooms or The Underbelly.

A Venue Site is a particular location within a Venue, e.g. The Pleasance Courtyard and The Pleasance Dome. Each Site has its own Venue Number.

A Stage is a particular theatre space within a Venue Site, e.g. The Wildman Room (Assembly) or The Debating Hall (The Gilded Balloon).

A particular Venue will often have many shows on each stage each day. The turn around time between shows is often 15-20 minutes. This means that if one show overruns, the rest of the shows for the day may do likewise. It's like flights from an airport. If the incoming flight is delayed, there is a knock on affect for the following flights. However, unless there is a technical problem (I mean at the Fringe, not at the airport), this is mainly likely to happen at the start of the Fringe when everyone (actors, technicians, etc.) is getting used to the process.

I set a personal record in 2006, having booked four shows in succession at The Assembly Rooms. What I did not realise at the time is that they were all in the same Stage. As each one finished, we filed out with the rest of the audience and joined the end of the queue for the next show. Unfortunately, you are not allowed to stay in your seats to wait for the next production. At least in this situation, if one show overruns, you cannot be late for the next one.

A situation that can be confusing is the fact that a particular Venue may change its physical location from year to year. I came unstuck one year when I booked a show at the Pod. The previous year, this had been located in a temporary structure at a site at the Festival Square on the Lothian Road. On arrival at the site, I was completely thrown to see an empty square. A glance at the programme confirmed that the Venue was now in Clerk Street, which is the other side of town. A quick taxi ride meant that we arrived just in time for the show and were rewarded with the "pleasure" of seeing one of only two shows that have ever scored zero on my personal scoring system. Since my scoring system is out of 10 rather than 5, this is no mean feat and has only ever been equalled by one other show on the fringe (See chapter 'Good, Bad and Ugly').

It appears that even seasoned Fringe attendees need to keep their wits about them.

Why Visit the Fringe

Why do you want to go to the Edinburgh Fringe Festival?

This may seem to be a basic question, but I think it is one that you need to ask yourself. The city is very busy during the Fringe Festival and you should perhaps go during this period only if you are going to make the most of the shows on offer or if you want to attend one of the other festivals that are on at the same time. If you think you will, perhaps, see a couple of Fringe shows and spend the rest of the time seeing the sights, visiting art galleries and the Castle, etc, then going to Edinburgh in the three weeks of the Fringe is not the best idea.

The cost alone should give you pause for thought. I go for six nights, flying up from London and staying in a medium class centrally located hotel. The total cost for two people including flights, accommodation, food, drink and shows is around £2000. This would be even higher if it were not for the fact that, due to the low cost airlines, the flights within the UK and Europe are cheap if you book far enough ahead.

A few of the Fringe Venues have shows all year round and it would be cheaper and less crowded to go at another time. In particular, if you want to see performances at the EIF, now that the Fringe weeks do not coincide, you should go in the last week, at the end of August and the beginning of September.

Along with many other people we go to the Fringe every year and I have recently been asking myself whether this is just habit or whether I truly want to go. In fact, having given it a bit of thought, I think that these days there is more reason to go than ever. In a week, I see a bigger variety of performances and talent than I would in a whole year of watching British television. In particular, the drama that is performed at the Fringe is often of the type and quality most people cannot see anywhere else. In 2006, three of the shows I saw were monologues lasting an hour or more, not the sort of thing that is going to be shown on prime time TV.

Underbelly Show Board in Bristo Square

One word of warning though. If you like it, prepared to be hooked. If you are coming from abroad, and there are many visitors from the USA and Japan, it may not be an option to come back. But if you live in the UK, an annual pilgrimage to the Fringe could be an option. There are plenty of people at the Fringe who come every year. Lots of them are locals. (Contrary to the rumours, not all the inhabitants of Edinburgh leave for the duration and rent out their homes for vast sums of money). Others like us come from other parts of the UK every year. We have bumped into the same woman, a casual acquaintance, at Edinburgh Airport three years running. Like us, she comes up to the Fringe every year at the same time.

The problems with this are the cost every year and, if you are not retired, taking a chunk of leave from work when you may have a lot of other things you want to do with your spare time.

When Is It Held

The Edinburgh Fringe Festival is held for around three weeks (23 days to be exact) in August, starting on a Sunday and ending on the last Monday of the month. Note that although this Monday is a Public Holiday in England, it is not a holiday in Scotland. Some Venues open a few days before the official start date to give preview performances of shows. For example, in 2007 The Pleasance started 4 days early on Wednesday the 1st August giving 27 days of performances.

So the decision you need to make is when to go.

I always go towards the end of the three weeks. I arrive on a Sunday and leave on the following Saturday, the last weekend of the Fringe. There are several advantages to this. Weekends are the busiest time at the Fringe. This is when the locals get the chance to see the shows, so everything is more crowded and it is more difficult to get tickets for some shows and get tables in restaurants. Also, by going towards the end of the Fringe, you will have more reviews to read and therefore more information on which to base your decisions as to what shows to book (See chapter 'What to See').

However, there are some reasons for going at other times. For most shows, the first couple of days are normally review days and you can get two tickets for the price of one. However, this is the time when the

Venues are getting their own organisation sorted out so you may find that the start times of shows are delayed.

If you are based in the UK and you do not want to take too much time off work, you can come up at the end of the Fringe, say Thursday morning, and go back Monday evening. You get four days at the Fringe, plus travelling time, for only two days off work, assuming that the Monday is a bank holiday.

As for the duration of the visit, that is going to depend entirely on personal preferences and the size of your wallet. I spend five and a half days watching the Fringe, packing in as many shows as possible, and go home feeling as if I need a week on the beach to recover. Other people stay longer and take a more relaxed approach to seeing shows.

Outside The Pleasance Courtyard

Personally, I feel that one can sit in a bar watching the world go by or stroll round an art gallery any time of the year in any city in the world. What I cannot do except for three weeks in August is enjoy the Edinburgh Fringe Festival. So my aim is always to pack in as much as possible in the available time and within my physical and financial capabilities.

How To Get There

Once you have decided that you are going to go to the Fringe (the easy bit), and when you are going, you need to decide how you are going to get to Edinburgh and where you are going to stay (more difficult, see next chapter).

For most people the options are limited to train or plane. For some, the car is an option, but I would suggest only for travel to and from Edinburgh. You will not need, and should not try to use, your car to get around the city during the Fringe (See chapter 'Getting Around'). Anyone living in the UK and more than perhaps a three or four hour drive from Edinburgh should use the train or plane.

If you live near an airport with direct flights to Edinburgh, this will probably be the preferred route. Not only is it the quickest, but it is currently the cheapest. I have just booked flights for next year and I could fly from London Heathrow to Edinburgh for £12 return plus tax. Unfortunately, the tax is nearly £60 but this still gives a total fare of around £70. I checked train fares for the same journey but unfortunately, they only seem to give train fares three months in advance so there is no direct comparison. However, the fare from London Euston to Edinburgh Waverley in November was around £100 if booked in advance.

At least with the train, you end up in the centre of the city. It should be a short bus or taxi ride to your hotel (If it isn't, your hotel is probably in the wrong place). With the plane, you will need to get to the

The Pleasance Courtyard Map

city centre using either the regular express bus service (£3) or by taxi (£15-£20 depending on the location of your hotel).

For the more adventurous types, you could take the sleeper train. Go to sleep in London at 11 o'clock in the evening and wake up in Edinburgh at 6.30 the next morning. (I am joking here. You will in fact wake up every time the train shudders to a stop en-route and every time your fellow travellers get up to go to the bathroom). Another issue here is what do you do in Edinburgh at 6.30 in the morning. When I tried this route many years ago, they allowed you stay on the train for a while when it arrived in Edinburgh but I do not know whether this is still the case.

Assuming you are booked into a hotel, your room is unlikely to be ready at that time in the morning, but you could just drop your bags off at reception, buy the local papers and start planning your day. There are Fringe shows in the morning but most of the ones before 11am are aimed at children (However, See chapter 'What to See').

Where To Stay

When it comes to accommodation, I can only pass on my favourite saying:

"You can never be too early; you can only be too late".

This normally applies to arriving at the airport for a flight, but it can equally apply to booking accommodation during the Fringe. (I am sure people can come up with many examples in life where this does not apply, but we are talking here about the principle).

Accommodation gets very booked up during the festivals in August, especially during the Fringe. It may always be possible to find some sort of place to stay, even at the last minute, but that takes no account of the cost, standard or location. It may be stating the obvious, but the earlier you book the more likely you are to get what you want at a price you can afford.

The most likely accommodation to consider is a hotel. These range from a typical business hotel with several hundred rooms to a privately run "bed and breakfast" establishment with 2 or 3 rooms. By necessity, the former is likely to be in the city centre and the latter somewhere in the suburbs. Each has its advantages. The large hotel will usually be centrally located and therefore convenient for access to the attractions.

It will also be useful if you need to pop back to the hotel for some reason during the day.

The down side is that you may be paying for service and facilities that you will not use.

I normally leave the hotel at 9.30 in the morning and return around midnight. I do not need a fully equipped gym or swimming pool. (If you still have the time and energy to use a gym while you are visiting the Fringe, you must be doing something wrong. Either that or you are much younger than me). All I need is a comfortable bed, clean bathroom and a decent breakfast in the morning.

This is probably as good time as any to mention the cleanliness of hotels in Edinburgh. I now have a low expectation of the standards. The hotels I have stayed in have been generally a bit grubby and "dog eared". Fixtures are broken and carpets worn. Perhaps I have been unlucky, but this has even been true of the more expensive hotels.

The worst place I have ever stayed in was the Café Royal hotel. I can name names since it no longer exists. Recently it has been converted into a back packers hostel (No surprise there then). We made the mistake of looking under the beds, not something I would recommend in any hotel in Edinburgh. It was not a pretty sight. It was the weekend and we could not find alternative accommodation until the Monday, but at the first opportunity, we checked out and booked into a different hotel on the outskirts of the city centre.

On another occasion, we stayed in a hotel two years running. On our second visit, following our experiences the previous year, my wife took a selection of cleaning materials in her case (bleach, scrubbing brush, etc.). She gave the bathroom a good cleaning before she would use it. The obvious question you are asking is why did we go back? Well when choosing a hotel in Edinburgh, my priorities and those of my wife are different. I want somewhere centrally located and value for money (not necessarily cheap but cheapish). She wants comfort and cleanliness. The compromise is that I can choose the hotel provided that she can give the room a spring clean when we arrive.

I may be being a bit harsh on the hotels in Edinburgh. The only time we stayed in a newish centrally located hotel it was fine and the small bed and breakfast places have generally been good. But since we want to stay in the centre of the city, the buildings are normally going to be old and this may contribute to the problem.

This general point may be confirmed by the fact that a relation of mine recently went to stay in a hotel near Inverness and she made the same comments, lovely place, beautiful view, grubby, tatty old hotel. Another friend has been to Scotland several times with his family to stay in a log cabin or a cottage. In spite of the fact that he drives there with a wife, three children and a dog, the wife insists that they take the Dyson vacuum cleaner. I said to my wife that this was a bit extreme, but she says that if it wasn't for the fact that we go by plane, she would take her Dyson to Edinburgh. My response to that is that if she takes her Dyson, I can take my power washer. I often sit outside in the city centre, see something and think that if only I had my Kracher with me, I could give it a good blast and it would come up lovely. Sometimes it's a building, other times a tourist.

Hang on; I seem to have gone "off piste". Let's get back to the point. (See chapter 'Getting Around' for another skiing analogy)

I have made a point about the hotels to set an expectation. And also, I may well have been unlucky. There are a lot of American tourists who stay in Edinburgh and they are not known for putting up with low standards of service. In fact, I may have answered my own question here. I used to book my accommodation in Edinburgh in January/February. But it was getting more and more difficult so I now book just before Christmas. Even then, many of the big modern hotels in the city centre seem to be fully booked. This may be because they are block booked by travel companies and therefore the ones that I can book are the ones that the travel companies do not want to use. This may also explain why a friend of mine managed to get a room in a large central hotel two weeks before the Fringe started when the same hotel was "fully booked" before Christmas. Travel companies may have released rooms that they did not need. I do not know for certain, I am only guessing.

The Udderbelly in Bristo Square

The small hotels on the outskirts of the city will probably require a bus or taxi ride, and therefore you may want to check a bus route map before you book such a place to make sure they are on or near a bus route. Getting a bus is not too difficult in the morning, but you may want to check whether there is a night bus service for the return journey. Of course, you may be able to get a taxi, but my experience is that they become scarce towards midnight and of course this is when the demand for taxis is greatest. I once walked several miles back to my accommodation, a journey that took over an hour. This may not seem a long time, but when you have spent a whole day walking around the city from Venue to Venue, it is not to be recommended.

Bear in mind that if you use a hotel in the city centre, it may be a bit noisy. Obviously there is the general traffic noise, but the festival activities go on until the wee small hours. To compound the problem, the street cleaners are out bright and early to clear up the mess from the night before. They need to do this before there are too many people on the streets.

When you book a hotel, check whether the price includes breakfast. If it doesn't, you will probably be better off going out for breakfast and you should make allowance for this if comparing prices. If breakfast is extra, it will often be expensive in a hotel. If you book a bed and breakfast hotel, it is worth checking when breakfast is served. I once stayed in one that only served breakfast between 8.00 and 8.30. I cannot help but think that this was designed to discourage guests and save on the cost of the food. This is borne out by the fact that on the one occasion I managed to get up in time, there were only two other people eating and this in a hotel that had 10 bedrooms.

There seem to be quite a few back packer hostels in Edinburgh but I have not had any experience of these establishments so I cannot comment on the availability or costs.

Another option when staying in Edinburgh is to rent a house or an apartment, the former for larger groups and the latter for as few a two people. However, this sort of accommodation can be difficult to find, especially at short notice. The people who put on shows at the Fringe often stay together in houses, which will work out cheaper on a per person/per night basis. For some shows, I suspect the entire company (actors, technicians, girl friends, etc.) stay in the same house, where the total number of people may or may not exceed the number of beds.

For this reason I doubt the oft quoted statement that many inhabitants of Edinburgh leave the city during the Fringe and rent their houses out for the duration. Personally, I would think twice before renting out my house during the Fringe regardless of how much rent I am offered. However, a figure of £10,000 per week would probably trigger that second thought. For anyone tempted at this price, the good news is that it is a very nice house. The bad news is that it fails the "It should be a short taxi ride from Waverley station" rule. It's just outside London.

Getting Around

It is several years since I travelled by bus or taxi in Edinburgh since the most convenient way to get around the city is on foot. The city centre area, which covers most of the Fringe Venues, is a fairly compact area. If you plan your shows carefully you can minimise the amount of walking. More importantly, you can minimise the amount of walking up or down hill.

For those unfamiliar with Edinburgh, the city centre is split between the Old Town, which radiates from the Royal Mile that runs east down from the Castle, and the New Town, which is the area to the North from Princes Street. (Here, Old and New are relative terms since the New Town was built more than 200 years ago). However, what both parts of the city have in common are hills and you should take account of this when moving around the city. My motto is "do not go up or down a hill unless you have to".

There may be some youngsters out there who cannot understand where I am coming from here. In fact, I cannot remember the hills being significant when I started visiting the Fringe many years ago. Now, as far as possible, I follow flat or flattish routes. In the New Town, this means roads parallel to Princes Street, i.e. east to west. In the Old Town, the corresponding roads run north to south (Lothian Road, George IV Bridge and North Bridge/South Bridge.

If you want to get around the New Town, it is best not walk along the pavements on Princes Street unless you have to. It is the main shopping

One of the Assembly Rooms Venues

street in the city and the pavements will be crowded. Princes Street is in fact one of the most attractive shopping streets in the world. The shops are on only one side of the street. The south side is a garden area with views to the Castle. You can avoid the crowds on the pavement by going into the gardens. Apart from where there are roads that cross the gardens, there are paths that run the length of Princes Street. These are wider and less crowded and, unless you are a keen shopper, the views are more appealing. In any case, if you want to do some shopping, there is a good craft market at the western end of the gardens, next to St John's church. There is another small market on the Royal Mile, just up on the left from the Fringe Office.

If you are going to Venues north of Princes Street, e.g. The Assembly Rooms or Hill Street Theatre, to travel east/west you can go along Rose Street, which has a lot of smaller shops and restaurants, or George Street.

In the Old Town, the best road to use is North Bridge/South Bridge. Many of the main Fringe Venues can be easily accessed from this road. In fact, the south east quadrant of the city (D5,E4/5/6,F6 area on the Fringe map) has more Venues and shows than any other area, so it would be a good idea to familiarise yourself with the area. If you want The Pleasance Courtyard, turn left off South Bridge and go via Drummond Street, Roxburgh Street and Adam Street. If you want the Pleasance Stages that are accessed from the street (Above, Below, Grand and Baby Grand), carry on straight down Drummond Street. This route avoids "Cardiac Hill", which is the part of The Pleasance road leading up from Cowgate. It doesn't seem too steep in the morning, but if you go to The Pleasance for a late show after a big meal, you may find this is a hill too far.

To get to Bristo Square (The Gilded Balloon, Udderbelly and The Pleasance Dome), go up North Bridge/South Bridge and turn right via Nicholson Square. This is particularly relevant if you are coming from the Fringe Office and you want to avoid the worst of the crowds. The High Street is closed to vehicles during the day and the road is full of street performers, and therefore crowds of onlookers. If you have time to push through the crowds or you want to stand and look, you can get to Bristo Square by going up the High Street and along George IV Bridge.

To give you an idea of how long it will take to walk between Venues, from the Traverse Theatre to The Pleasance Courtyard is about 35 minutes and from The Pleasance Courtyard to The Assembly Rooms about 25 minutes. If you look at the Fringe map, you can use these times to gauge the walking times between other Venues.

At this point, it's probably worth mentioning an oddity in the Old town. On the Fringe map, North Bridge and George IV Bridge both cross Cowgate, but note that these roads are at different levels. There is no access from either bridge to Cowgate unless you go through the Venue Site called The Underbelly, (See chapter 'Venues'). The same applies where North Bridge crosses Market Street and Johnston Terrace goes over King's Stables Road.

This explains some of the hills in the area. If South Bridge goes over Cowgate but links up with the High Street, all the roads linking Cowgate with the High Street must involve a significant incline.

Sorry to go on about these hills, but for someone my age it's important, especially on "Ski Wednesday".

This is a phenomenon I encountered when I used to go skiing. A typical UK package skiing holiday would run from Saturday to Saturday and I used to notice that skiing on the Wednesday was the most problematic. The legs ached and the blisters were starting to cause problems. This was particularly true for me; someone who used to do very little physical exercise during the rest of the year but then decided to jump from the top of a mountain all day, every day, for a week. I would have more falls on "Ski Wednesday" than all the other days put together. When Thursday came round, the aches had receded and the skiing improved. "Ski Wednesday" was like "hitting the wall" during the marathon. You just had to get through it. I noticed the same effect when I had a skiing holiday from Sunday to Sunday, but it occurred on the Thursday. However, to save confusion it was still called "Ski Wednesday".

During a visit to the Fringe, if I arrive at lunchtime on Sunday, "Ski Wednesday" occurs on Wednesday, which is convenient. The legs start to ache and sometimes a trip to the chemist/pharmacy is required to get plasters for the blisters. In fact, this is a good time to discuss clothing and footwear for the Fringe.

Footwear is the most important area of clothing to consider. If you do a lot of walking around in Edinburgh, you are going to need something suitable. This is especially important where the roads and pavements are cobbled, which is often the case in Edinburgh. This includes The Pleasance Courtyard. Bear in mind that if you twist or break an ankle, the disabled access to many Venues is not good and for the ladies, it will make "hovering" near impossible (see chapter 'Getting to the Show' regarding toilets).

Also, in the event that it rains, you do not want to get wet feet when it may be hours before you get back to the hotel. So, even though it is summer, the best option is a decent pair of lace up walking shoes or boots. (Note to the Ladies: When it comes to clothing and footwear for the Fringe, put practicality before style and fashion or you may live to regret it. It cannot be a coincidence that many "Ladies of the Night" in Edinburgh wear Doc Martins). You want something that holds your feet and does not allow them to slide around. For example, last year I wore a pair of slip on shoes that seemed perfectly comfortable. What I did not realise was that the heel slipped up and down as I walked. Normally, this was not a problem, but I probably do more walking in one week at the Fringe than in the rest of the year and the heel blisters appeared within a couple of days.

As for clothing, we need to consider the climate in Edinburgh during the Fringe and the practical requirements.

In Edinburgh in the summer, you can encounter any sort of climatic condition, except snow (and even that I'm not absolutely sure about).

Princes Street Gardens

However, although for most summer holidays a clear sunny day would be ideal, this is not so for the Fringe. You will be doing a lot of walking, which will work up a sweat in the heat, and the Venues can be uncomfortable if it is hot (See chapter 'The Venues'). The ideal is that the days are mainly cloudy but it is not raining and the temperature is around 20ºC and luckily that is the case for much of the time during the Fringe.

If you can, check the weather forecast for the day before you set out in the morning. You do not want to be wearing several layers of clothing if it turns out to be warm. Likewise, you do not want to be wearing a skimpy little number if the weather turns hostile. As a male, I find that the best option is to wear a single top with a top pocket (T-Shirt or Shirt) and a lightweight jacket. This should have plenty of closable pockets but something that you do not mind folding up and putting under you seat while you are watching a show. (Hence the closable pockets to stop things falling out). If it is waterproof, so much the better, but if not, don't worry.

In my experience, it is rare but not unknown that it will rain all day at the Fringe. More likely there will be the odd shower. On a six day trip to the Fringe, I'd expect a bit of rain on one or two days. If it does rain, I will cope with it at the time, either by sheltering until it passes or by buying an umbrella. We do not carry an umbrella around all the time. If it is an umbrella big enough for two, you cannot put it in a hand bag or pocket and you will probably leave it somewhere by mistake. If it is small enough to get in a bag, it won't be big enough for two. I have so many tartan umbrellas at home now that if I do need to buy another one while I am at the Fringe, I normally leave it in the hotel room.

If you are going to a show that is held in the open air, you may want to purchase a cagoule (plastic mac with hood that slips over the head). These fold up very small and can easily fit into a hand bag or pocket. They are particularly useful if you go to the Tattoo. They sell them in many of the tourist shops including the Tattoo shop, which is on Market Street next to Waverley Station and is marked "C" on the Fringe Programme map. It is not particularly practical to use an umbrella at a show, at least it isn't for the person sitting behind you.

Lastly, we need to cover the subject of hand bags. If you are going to go to the Fringe, the best companion (wife/girlfriend/boyfriend) you can have is one with a large hand bag. It should be at least "A4" size, i.e. big enough to hold the Fringe programme.

It may be worth while going through a list of the things that we (but mainly the wife) carry around at the Fringe:

Tickets
I only carry around the tickets for today's shows, just in case I lose them.

Fringe Programme
These are free and are widely available but we make notes on ours so we always carry our own copy with us.

Map of Edinburgh
The map in the Fringe Programme does not detail all the roads. (In fact as I write this, I am not sure why we carry this around. I cannot remember the last time we referred to it).

Latest Scotsman Review Section
To be read so that my personal list can be updated (see below).

Latest Metro Review Section
Ditto

Daily Diary
Free version sponsored (in 2007) by the Guardian is the best.

Chronological List of Potential Shows
This is my personal list that I started drawing up before coming to the Fringe.

Chronological List of Booked Shows
So you know what you are doing next.

Pages from Restaurant Listing

I buy the Restaurant Listing published by the List magazine and tear out the pages that refer to the centre of Edinburgh (I have just realised why I have the map of Edinburgh. Not all the roads are marked on the map in the Fringe Programme).

Mobile Phones

We use these to call Venues in order to buy tickets and restaurants to reserve tables. But keep them on silent/vibrate for the duration of the Fringe to save you having to switch them off for each show. If it does ring during a performance, heaven help you, especially if you are sitting near the front watching a stand-up comedian.

Wet Wipes

There will be things you do not want to sit on or eat off of before you have cleaned them.

Tissues

Ditto, and in case you get a sneezing fit during a show.

Pens

You will be making a lot of notes.

Mints/Cough Drops

In case you start coughing during a performance.

Tooth Picks

In case you are in a hurry and you do not have time to pick out the debris in the restaurant.

Pain Killers

If you are in a loud show and you are seated next to the speakers.

Indigestion Tablets
If you have rushed your meal you will probably need these.

Plasters
These are mainly for blisters. The fabric type give more cushioning effect but if the blister is small or for corns, the small padded ones with the hole in the middle are best.

Reading Glasses
Even if you think your vision is good, some of the print is very small. The Fringe Programme map index and the Scotsman Daily Diary spring to mind. Keep them handy in the pocket of your shirt (Now you know why).

Cagoules
Only if you have bought one but you haven't used it yet. If you have, it will take ages to dry out and you will never fold it up a small as it was when you bought it.

These items are obviously in addition to the normal things one may carry around. I have included the Fringe Programme although this last year I was surprised how little I actually referred to it. When you are out and about, a copy of the Scotsman Daily Diary may be enough and you can always find a Fringe programme if you need one.

For those of you who think you will use a rucksack instead of a hand bag, my advice is, don't. For a start, if you are a man you will probably have to carry it. If you use a hand bag, it will be the wife/girlfriend who acts as the sherpa. (I find it pays if you occasionally offer to carry the hand bag. Such a gesture goes down well with the ladies. She probably won't accept, since she won't trust you to look after it. If she does, leave it unattended somewhere. She won't let you carry it again).

I also object to rucksacks from a practical point of view. Someone wearing a rucksack takes up a bigger footprint than those who don't. Edinburgh is crowded enough as it is without people taking up more than their fair share of space. Bear in mind that if everyone in the queue for a sold out show in the Dance Hall at The Assembly Rooms was wearing a rucksack, the end of the Queue would be the Gorbals. And that's before they swing it off their shoulder. As for couples who are both wearing rucksacks, well just don't get me started........

(PS Yes I know the Gorbals is in Glasgow, it's a sort of joke).

I have assumed so far that you will be walking around the City, but there are occasions when you may need to get a taxi or bus.

All the "hailable" taxis in Edinburgh (i.e. those you can flag down in the street) are of the black "London Taxi" style. They can take up to five passengers and are all wheel chair accessible. Taxis are at a premium during the Fringe and depending on the time of day, it may be difficult to get one. However, there is often a queue of them waiting outside the bigger Venues at peak times (The Pleasance and The Assembly Rooms). If you want to get somewhere quickly the taxi is an option even though the roads are busy. The driver will know the quickest route.

The buses are another option, but in the main they follow the principle roads around the city and these are the busiest. In the past, it has been quicker to walk than get a bus, certainly along Princes Street. However, in recent years parts of Princes Street have been closed for cars and this has made the buses much quicker.

You can buy the day ticket on the bus and the price is £2.50 (2007). There are other ticket options on the Lothian Buses Web site. Note that some of the buses are not run by Lothian Buses and so the day ticket may not be accepted on all buses.

The Venues

The shows on the Fringe are held at various Venues in and around the city. In fact, just a few are well outside the city. Rosslyn Chapel, of "The Da Vinci Code" fame, was listed as a Venue in 2007 and it is 7 miles from the city centre. But even that can be beaten. Both Traquair House and Stenton Gallery are about 30 miles from the centre.

However, these are the exceptions. Most Venues are in the city centre and of those, the greatest concentration of shows is held in the area to the south east of the castle.

In 2007 there were over 250 Venues and they can vary from multi-stage buildings, which are open all year round, to single stage in a church or hotel meeting rooms that revert to their normal use when the Fringe is over. The range of options for Venues is enormous. They also vary from year to year. Small Venues may exist one year but disappear the next. This, together with the nature of some Venues, (attics, basements, etc) makes it difficult always to provide disabled access. However, where reasonable, the Fringe is committed to providing the best access possible. For particular information, you should contact the individual Venues concerned.

In an increasing trend, the larger Venues are using multiple sites. The Pleasance has the main Courtyard site and The Pleasance Dome near Bristo Square. The Assembly has the main Site in George Street, but in

2007 it also had 7 other Sites. This can be confusing when buying tickets so make sure that you know exactly which Site you need to head for to see a particular show. Sometimes, these are new Sites for the Fringe, other times The Assembly has taken an existing Venue under its wing, e.g. Hill Street Theatre. Whether in the long term this benefits the Sites in terms of ticket sales remains to be seen. Each site is given a separate Venue Number in the Programme, but you still need be to be careful and check exactly where you need to go to see a show.

The Pleasance Dome

It's even more important when you are planning what you are going to see. You may think you have booked 2 shows at the same Venue, where the second one starts a half an hour after the first one ends, only to find the second one is at a different Site 15 minutes walk away.

In 2007, of the 8 Venues Sites under The Assembly Rooms banner, 3 were called "Assembly@George Street", "Assembly@St George's West" and "Assembly@Assembly Hall". It's as if they have set out deliberately to confuse. Likewise, The Underbelly had 5 Venues Sites, two of which are called "The Underbelly" and "The Udderbelly". Clever play on words or just confusing? To make matters worse, they insist on one of their Venues Sites, The Smirnoff Baby Belly, being listed under the letter "U" in the programme. (This Venue Site used to be part of The Gilded Balloon). The name of this Venue Site also indicates another trend, Venue sponsorship.

The moral of this story is, "Check the Venue Site".

In order to locate a Venue, you can use the map at the back of the Fringe programme. It lists the Venues alphabetically and by Venue number. The Fringe Web site does not include maps.

In 2007, there were over 200 Venues used for the Fringe shows. In fact, I counted 233 in the Fringe Programme but after the event, the Fringe Web site says that there were 261. It is possible that some were added after the programme was printed. This certainly happens with individual shows (See chapter 'What To See').

However, there are a few "mega" Venues that between them probably put on more performances than all the others put together. They are also there year after year, so it is worth mentioning them specifically. These include what I refer to as the "big 4", these being The Pleasance, The Gilded Balloon, The Assembly Rooms and The Underbelly. In theory, you can book tickets for all these Venues in person through each of their box offices (not online) although twice when I tried to pick up tickets for a different Venue (Assembly tickets at The Pleasance and Underbelly tickets at The Gilded Balloon) I was told it was not possible.

(The numbers in brackets after the title are the Venue Numbers for the main Site).

The Pleasance (33)

This Venue has 2 sites, The Pleasance Courtyard and The Pleasance Dome. The Pleasance Courtyard is the main Site. It is a collection of buildings around a courtyard and takes its name from the road on which it is situated. It is owned by the university but during the Fringe, it is taken over by The Pleasance Trust, which is a charity. In Edinburgh, the trust only puts on shows during the Fringe but it has opened a similar Venue in London that is a permanent site for entertainment and is open all year round.

It is probably the most attractive of the main Venues, since the style of the buildings and the courtyard make an attractive setting for drinking and eating outside. The second site, The Pleasance Dome on Bristo Square, is also part of the university.

The Pleasance is the biggest Venue at the Fringe. In 2007, it sold over 270,000 tickets. If you consider that the whole Fringe sold around 1.7 million, then The Pleasance accounts for nearly 1 in 6 of all the tickets sold. No surprise, since it had 20 stages and put on more than 185 shows for 4,500 performances. There were more than 1,000 performers involved. Until I started writing this book, I assumed that The Pleasance was open all year round, like the one in London. I am amazed to think that this whole enterprise is open just for three and a half weeks in August.

Once I had seen these figures, I checked the shows that I had seen in the last couple of years. In 2006, of 31 shows, 10 were at The Pleasance. In 2007 it was 15 out of 32 shows. That was in spite of the fact that I had tried to find other Venues to visit, just for a change. But with the variety of shows and the calibre of the acts, it is difficult to venture far away from The Pleasance

Although the shows at The Pleasance cover a broad range, it is comedy for which it is well know. In 2007, all of the 5 main nominees for the Fringe Eddies comedy awards were performing at The Pleasance. In 2007, of the 187 shows listed in the Fringe programme for The Pleasance, Comedy was the largest group with 118. Theatre had 49 and the other 18 was Kids, Music, Opera and Dance. Comedy, in its various guises, therefore represented 64% of the entire programme.

During the Fringe, The Courtyard site has more than a dozen stages available, some of which will be showing performances from before midday to after midnight. They range in seating capacity from 50 to the largest, The Pleasance Grand, which I believe is in a sports hall, seats 750. A list of the shows for the day is indicated on a large show board above the courtyard, stage by stage in chronological order.

Apart from The Pleasance Grand, the other large stages are Pleasance Beyond and Pleasance One. The latter suffers from a problem that is perhaps unique to The Pleasance, padded bench seats. They are designed to hold anything up to 12 people each but the seating area for each person is not marked, so you do not have any idea how much room you are supposed to have. The first 5 minutes of each show involves Pleasance staff telling people to shimmy up closer so that all the audience can get in. The Pleasance Above is the same, as is The Pleasance Cavern and the "Freight Container" rooms such as The Hut. Pleasance One also suffers from the fact that many of the seats are on the level, only the rear seats are raked.

The other stages at the Courtyard are:

Medium Size (100-200 seats): Pleasance Two, Cabaret Bar, Cavern, Upstairs and Above

Small Size (50-100 seats): Baby Grand, Beside, Attic, Below, Hut and Cellar

The Pleasance Hut

In 2007, at least 3 of the small stages (Baby Grand, Beside and Hut) were in temporary rooms made up of freight containers stuck together. They are dismantled and removed at the end of the Fringe. They can present a problem when the weather is warm. They can get very hot and uncomfortable. In very hot weather, the Venue does install air conditioning units, but in a small space, the noise can be intrusive. The heat can also be a problem in stages situated in the roof space, i.e. The Attic. In these conditions you may want to keep a bottle of water handy.

The Courtyard has many bars, which serve food and drink all day, and a lot of seating, much of it outside. This provides a very attractive area in which to congregate, particularly in the afternoon. In the evening, it becomes crowded when the locals turn up, especially if the weather is fine. Even so, the Venue seems to cope with the numbers.

Food is served in the bar that is to the right as you go in the main entrance towards The Pleasance One Stage, where the box office is to the left. There is also a temporary structure selling cold food on the opposite side of the courtyard facing The Pleasance Beside Stage. If you want a quiet place to sit, you could try the Wine Bar, which is up a short flight of steps to the right as you go through the main archway from the street.

The box office is on the left as you go through the main archway entrance and is not really big enough for the size of the Venue, particularly at weekends. If you have pre-booked tickets by phone or on the Web, you should pick them up from the booth on the right in the Courtyard. If you are going to queue for tickets, check the blackboard on the left as you go through the arch into the courtyard. It will list shows that are sold out. This is particularly relevant at the weekend and in the evening when The Pleasance is very busy. You do not want to queue for half an hour only to find out that the show you want to see is sold out.

If you need to locate your particular Pleasance Stage, there is a sign post in the middle of the courtyard and in 2007 there was a large illuminated map at the main entrance on the left just after the box office. The entrance to The Pleasance Above and Pleasance Below stages is in the street 20 metres down from the main entrance. The entrance to Pleasance Grand and Baby Grand is a further 40 meters down the hill although there is a back route from the courtyard if you go past The Hut stage and keep going. This is also where you can find the main gents toilets (20 standing 6 seated), which are a better option than the ones in the basement of the main building (4 standing 2 seated). The latter are on the left past the box office.

The second Pleasance site is The Pleasance Dome (Venue 23). In 2007, this had 6 stages, 3 medium (Ace Dome, King Dome and Queen Dome) and 3 small (Jack Dome, 10 Dome and Joker Dome). They are situated around an indoor courtyard with food and drink available all day. The box office is on the right as you enter through the main entrance. There is no outside seating and it is a 5-7 minute walk from The Pleasance Courtyard.

The Pleasance publishes a joint programme with The Assembly Rooms.

The Assembly Rooms (3)

As previously mentioned, The Assembly Rooms had 8 Venue Sites in 2007. Some (Hill Street Theatre and Universal Arts) were relatively close to the main Venue Site but others were a 10-15 minute walk away. The furthest was the Queen's Hall, which is a brisk 30-40 minutes. For this section, I am only going to cover the main Venue Site on George Street.

This Site is housed in an elegant Georgian building, typical of the area on the south side of George Street. The size of the frontage belies the size of the Venue. There are 6 stages and the average number of seats is greater than The Pleasance. They are:

Large Size: The Music Hall (750 seats) and The Ballroom (341)

Medium Size: The Supper Room (150), The Edinburgh Suite (156), The Wildman Room (122), The Drawing Room (96)

The box office and ticket collection point are in a temporary structure down the alley to the left as you face the building. The list of today's shows is at the entrance to the alley. It is chalked on a small blackboard at ground level and is not easy to see, particularly when people walk in front of it on their way to the box office. Also, the writing tends to disappear if it rains. The Assembly Rooms could do with designing a more accessible show board like The Pleasance and The Underbelly. There is an information desk to the left in the main foyer.

The queues for the Ballroom and Music Hall are formed in the street. The Ballroom is the queue to the right as you face the building, the Music Hall to the left. The Wildman Room queue forms to the right in the foyer and snakes back down the steps to the right towards the alley. The queue for the Drawing Room starts on the first floor.

The Edinburgh Suite and the Supper Room are at the back of the building. They can be accessed through the foyer, turn right down the steps and into the alley then turn left. They can be accessed more easily directly from Rose Street. The queue for the Edinburgh Suite goes round into Rose Street, the one for the Supper Room goes up the alley.

Although The Assembly Rooms has fewer stages than The Pleasance, they are less ramshackle. There is proper seating in all the theatres (no benches) and seem more comfortable. The overall effect befits the style of the building. As with The Pleasance, it is only open as an entertainment Venue during the Fringe.

However, what it gains in style it looses in refreshment options. There are just two bars serving drink and a limited range of food and very little outside seating, just a couple of wooden benches on the street. The bar that serves these tables is the one through the glass fronted archway to right as you look at the building. The large glass doors give a certain open air feeling. The food is limited to sandwiches and toasted paninis. The limited table space and small uncomfortable chairs mean it is not the sort of place to linger for too long. However, it can be a pleasant place to spend time late morning while making decisions about shows. The other bar is at the rear of the building on the first floor. It is a windowless room but it does have a few computers for Internet access. There are gents' toilets on the ground floor on the left after the information desk (5 standing, 1 seated) or on the first floor (12 standing, 2 seated).

However, whereas The Pleasance is on the edge of the city centre, The Assembly Rooms are in the centre and there are plenty of restaurants and bars in the surrounding area, particularly Rose Street.

In 2007, for all Assembly Sites, the 142 shows were made up of Theatre 55, Comedy 39, Music 21, Dance 18 and Children's Shows 9. Here, Comedy is just 27% of the total. However, these figures are distorted by the new Venue sites that have been absorbed into The Assembly family. For Example, of the 18 Dance shows, 15 were performed at Aurora Nova and only one at the main site on George Street. In fact the figures for the latter are Theatre 25, Comedy 23, Music 3, Dance 1 and Children's Shows 6, so Comedy represented 43% of the total.

The Gilded Balloon (14)

Together with The Pleasance and The Assembly Rooms, The Gilded Balloon was one of the original "big 3" of the Edinburgh Fringe. Together, they published a joint Fringe programme and enjoyed the lion's share of the ticket sales. In 2002, things changed. The main Gilded Balloon building in Cowgate was destroyed by fire but luckily for The

Gilded Balloon, at the previous Fringe they had expanded their operation into the Teviot Hall University building on Bristo Square. This has been the base for their operations every year since and of the current "big 4" (now including The Underbelly), The Gilded Balloon is the only one that operates from a single site. It works in conjunction with The Underbelly, including the publication of a joint programme.

When The Gilded Balloon first moved, Bristo Square was in Fringe terms a bit of a backwater. But with The Pleasance Dome and in 2006, the introduction of the Udderbelly (see below), the area is now much more vibrant. With the Spiegeltent now in the Edinburgh Gardens, just behind the Teviot building, the centre of gravity for the Fringe has somehow moved south east. This is partly due to the option of providing space for outdoor eating and drinking in this area.

The Gilded Balloon has an outdoor seating area to the left as you face the building. There are various stalls offering food and a bar. Opposite, The Underbelly Site offers similar options. Indoors, there is a bar on the first floor and a café serving food and drink on the ground floor. There are toilets in the basement but it is easier to use the ones in the south east corner of The Underbelly courtyard. The building faces Bristo Square and access to all the Stages is through the main entrance, as is the Box Office and ticket collection point, which is facing you as you enter the building.

The list of today's programmes and sold out shows is chalked on a series of blackboards on railings either side of the entrance. Like The Assembly Rooms, they are not easy to see. For busy shows in the large Stages, the queues form outside the main entrance.

There are 8 Stages at The Gilded Balloon. These are:

Large Size: Debating Hall (350 seats)

Medium Size: Wine Bar (160), Night Club (150), Dining Room (120)

Small Size: Sportsmans (80), Billiard Room (60), Balcony (60), Wee Room (50)

Like The Assembly Rooms there is proper seating in all the theatres (no benches) and they seem more comfortable than some at The Pleasance. Like the other Venues mentioned, it is only open as an entertainment Venue during the Fringe.

If you want to eat there are plenty of restaurants and bars in the surrounding area, particularly to the north and east, on Potterrow and beyond to Nicholson Street.

In 2007 the 88 shows were made up of Theatre 21, Comedy 60, Music 3, and Children's Shows 4. Comedy represents 68% of the total, which is even higher than The Pleasance.

The Gilded Balloon produces a joint programme in conjunction with The Underbelly.

The Underbelly (61)

The Underbelly is the newest of the "big 4" Venues having been founded as recently as 2000. That first year it was part of the "C" Venue but since 2001 it has been run as a separate operation. The operation has expanded and The Underbelly now has 3 Sites with the addition of the

Baby Belly (in "caves" that were formally part of The Gilded Balloon) and the Udderbelly Pasture made up of the Udderbelly and the Cowbarn in Bristol Square.

Its main building is arranged over three floors that were formerly bank vaults under the Central Library. They are perhaps the most interesting base for any of the main Fringe Venues. However, the organisation of the building makes disabled access very difficult. Even "abled" access can be tricky with old stone spiral staircases giving access to some of the Stages. The building is odd in that access can be from the main entrance on the ground floor on Cowgate or from the top floor, which is on the corner of Victoria Street and George IV Bridge. Once you are inside the building you have the impression of being in a cave, due in part to the musty atmosphere and the absence of any windows.

The Underbelly Site has 4 bars, one of which is outside although not exactly in the open air since it is in the high ceiling "tunnel" that forms the main entrance off Cowgate. This is where the main box office is situated. The list of today's shows is posted on a large high level board mounted on the wall opposite the box office. There is a secondary box office at the entrance on the top floor.

There are 7 Stages at The Underbelly Site. These are:

Medium Size: White Belly (185), Belly Laugh (125), Belly Button (100)

Small Size: Belly Dancer (70) Iron Belly (60), Big Belly (60), Dehli Belly (50)

The Stages I have visited at The Underbelly all have separate seats rather than benches. As with The Pleasance, it is only open as an entertainment Venue during the Fringe.

To eat, the best option in the area is to turn right out of the main entrance and go along to The Grassmarket, the right hand side of which is lined with restaurants

The Baby Belly site (Venue 88) can be located by turning left out of the main entrance. It is about a 5 minute walk away and has 5 stages named "Baby Belly 1" to "Baby Belly 5". (I guess it was difficult to come up with any more names with "Belly" in the title). There is a box office and a bar.

The Udderbelly Pasture (Venue 300) is made up of two Sites in and around Bristo Square, each housing one Stage. The Udderbelly is a temporary structure in the shape of an upside down plastic purple cow (sic). Seating 322 it is the largest of The Underbelly Stages. The "pasture" is made up of a green carpet that is laid on the ground outside the Venue. Excluding grass, it is one of the few areas of Edinburgh where you may consider sitting on the ground, at least in the first few days of the Fringe before it has been "worn in". Bars food stalls and toilets (10 standing 3 seated) are arranged around the edge of an outdoor seating area.

The other Site is the Cowbarn, which shares the same Venue number even though it is a different building. It is housed in the Reid Hall Concert Hall, which is next to The Gilded Balloon building. It seats 230 and although it does not have its own bar, it is close enough to the Udderbelly and Gilded Balloon facilities for this not to be a problem.

The box office and ticket collection point is on the west side of Bristo Square next to a large high level sign giving details of today's shows at all The Underbelly Stages.

In 2007, The Underbelly Sites staged 136 shows made up of Comedy 61, Theatre 52, Music 6, Children's Shows 5 and Dance 2 giving Comedy 45% of the total.

C" (34)

The "C" Venue has been around since 1992 when it started at a Site on Princes Street. It subsequently moved to its current base in 2000 and has continued to grow in size every year since. In 2007 it was spread over 8 Sites. However, it does not yet have the profile of the "big 4" Venues. This is partly due to its laudable policy of concentrating on drama, particularly new writing. Also, it does not share its marketing and booking systems with any other Venues.

Its main Site, "C", is on 5 floors of a building on Chambers Street. It is unusual in that there is lift access to all the Stages. The box office and information desk are facing you as you go through the entrance with the entrance to the bar in the middle. There are flat screen signs above the desks giving details of shows for today, rather in the style of an airport departures screen. However, they only show the ones due to start in the next hour or so and therefore are not as useful as other Venues when planning the day ahead.

The bar is pretty soulless and not a place in which to linger. This has been a problem for this Venue for some time in that there is no outside space. However this was solved, at least in 2007, by extending the Site into the vacant land behind the building. This land used to house The Gilded Balloon before it burnt down. Although designated as a separate Venue Site, "C" Soco, it was connected to the main Venue Site by a rear door down the stairs to the right as you enter the main building. This offered outdoor seating and a café serving food and drink as well as additional performance spaces. However, this land will be redeveloped at some stage and presumably this extension will no longer be an option. There are gents' toilets on the basement level down both the left hand staircase (4 standing 4 seated) and right hand staircase (3 standing 3 seated).

There are 4 Stages at the main "C" Site; apart from the entrance level there is one on each floor. They are all medium sized seating between 100-200 people. They are imaginatively named C+1, C+2, C+3 and C-1 to indicate which floor they are on. They all have separate seats rather than benches.

To eat, you can either turn right out of the main entrance and then left along King George IV Bridge or left and then right along South Bridge.

The other sites are all relatively close to the main Site (C Baraka and C central 2 minutes walk, C Too and C Cubed 5-10 minutes walk). The exception in 2007 was Craigmillar Castle, which was several miles away. There was no public transport so the Venue ran a coach service from the main Site.

In 2007, the "C" Sites staged 157 shows made up of Comedy 15, Theatre 80, Music and Musicals 31, Children's Shows 19 and Dance 12 giving Comedy less than 10% of the total. This confirms that fact that the "C" Venue does not have the same performance profile as the "Big 4", even though in 2007 it put on more shows than any of them, with the exception of The Pleasance.

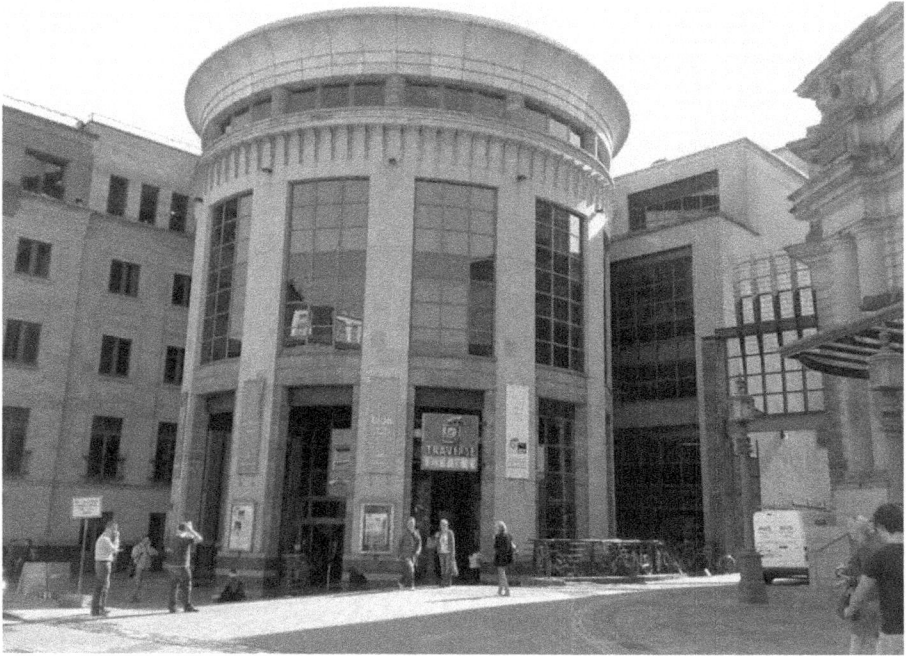

Traverse (15)

Being a proper theatre, The Traverse is one on the few Fringe Venues that is open all year round and this is one of the many aspects that sets the Traverse apart. It concentrates solely on drama and in some cases it commissions pieces from its own production company, which develops shows not only for performance in Edinburgh but worldwide.

Other respects that make it different are the duration and start times of shows. The theatre pieces tend to be of normal length, i.e. 2-2½ hours with an intermission. Typical drama shows on the Fringe are 1-1½ hours with no break. And whereas most shows on the Fringe start at the same time every day, in order to give each show a fair crack at the peak times, the Traverse mixes the start times. A show may start at 11:00am one day and 8:00pm the next. The disadvantage of this approach is that it is difficult to put Traverse shows on a chronological list by start time, at least one that applies to every day of the week.

However, one big advantage is that you can see a show with a long duration without eating into core dining and viewing time in the evening. If you go to see a 2½ hour show starting at 8:00pm, that's pretty much the rest of the evening written off. However, see the same show at 11:00am and you finish in time for lunch, having got a decent piece of theatre under your belt.

The quality of the shows at the Traverse also tends to be more reliable and the Venue regularly picks up awards during the Fringe, particularly Fringe First Awards. This is one reason why the shows at the Traverse tend to get booked up quickly, so you need to buy your tickets at the earliest opportunity. However, in general the tickets at The Traverse are also more expensive than other Venues.

The main Site is on Cambridge Street and again, unlike most Fringe Venues, it is housed in a modern building. There are 2 Stages. Traverse 1 is the main Stage seating up to 350 and Traverse 2 up to 100. The seating is odd. The seats in Traverse 1 are like padded benches with backrests where the seat folds up, but to do this you have to get synchronised with everyone else sharing the same seat. The seats in Traverse 2 are like padded shelves. The box office is at the end of the foyer area, opposite the entrance.

There is a decent bar/café that serves good food, at least relative to other Venues. This is probably because it is a permanent Venue with long term catering staff. However, it is in a mainly windowless room so it is not somewhere where you are going to spend a long time hanging around. There is no outside seating. There are toilets on the same level as the bar, to the right of the right hand entrance to Traverse 1. (I do not have the standing/seated figures. I had been getting some strange looks from people when I went into a Gents toilet, scrutinised the options and left without availing myself of the facilities, so I stopped. My wife was also getting a bit suspicious).

In common with other Venues, The Traverse has introduced satellite sites. Originally these were one show sites but in 2007 Traverse 3 at the university Drill Hall was hosting 5 shows, again starting at different times each day. The other Sites were Traverse at The Fruitmarket Gallery (Traverse 4?) and Traverse 5, which is at the Medical School. In each case, these Sites are 20-30 minutes walk from the main Site.

In 2007, the Traverse staged 19 shows over the 4 Sites and won 5 of the 116 Fringe First awards for drama.

The Spiegel Garden (87)

The George Square Gardens, south of Bristo Square, houses one of the most attractive and unusual Venues on the Fringe, The Spiegel Garden featuring The Spiegeltent. The Tent used to be housed on Princes Street above Waverley station but the move to the current site has opened up many options for the Venue, including for the first time an additional performance space in the Bosco Theater.

The Spiegeltent is a temporary structure made not entirely of canvas, as the name would suggest, but also of wood and mirrored glass. It was built in 1920 and its appearance is a combination of fair ground and music hall. Indeed the Venue fosters this feeling with sideshows in the Gardens (2007 included The Insect Circus Museum and a Freak Show) and the Venue staff dressed up in costume like fairground spielers.

Inside, the Speigeltent has a night club/circus feel to it. The centre has tables and chairs while fixed booths seating 8 or more people line the walls. If you are at the front of the queue and you end up sitting in the middle of the bench, you will disturb a lot of people if you want to get out, so "make yourself comfortable" before you go in. There is a bar inside the Spiegeltent and it is open during most performances. Overall, it is just about the best Venue space for the late night revue type of show.

The Bosco Theater is a new addition to the Spiegel Garden. It is even older than the Spiegeltent, dating from 1909. It was originally used for circus performances, although judging by its small size I can only imagine that there were no elephants or trapeze artists in the shows. It has the dubious distinction of having the smallest most uncomfortable seats of any Fringe Venue I have ever visited. They are wooden benches about 10" deep and unpadded. The limited leg room means you cannot shift forward to get your bottom on the seat, you just perch on the middle of your thighs. Luckily, the show I saw in the Bosco Theater in 2007 only lasted an hour.

The queues for both Stages form outside the buildings, stretching across the Gardens. The box office is on the right at the entrance to the Venue and there is outside seating with bars and food outlets in the Gardens.

What To See

Of all the decisions you have to make regarding the Fringe, the question of what to see is going to be the most important. After all, the whole point of coming to the festival is to see the performances. Unfortunately, and assuming that you want something entertaining and memorable, this is also the most difficult.

Of course you could make the decision process very simple by just sticking a pin in random pages of the Fringe programme. Having tried various methods of selecting shows, none of which have proved particularly reliable, I have considered this option but I have not been brave enough to try it yet.

Anyway, here are the various options that can assist you.

Fringe Programme

The reference point for shows at the Fringe is the Fringe Festival programme. This is published in June and is free. If you want to get a copy as soon as it is published, register on the Fringe Web site in May or join the 'Friends of the Fringe' scheme. You will then receive the programme through the post as soon as it is available.

The programme contains details of all the shows that will be performed at the Fringe, or at least those that were known at the date of publication. Shows are often added after publication date and some are cancelled after the programme has been printed. The programme is divided into alphabetic sections by type of show, i.e., comedy, theatre, etc. The performers make the decision as to which section the show goes into so a piece of theatre that includes comedy can be in either the Comedy or the Theatre section. There is an index by show title across all genres.

The entry for each show includes the Venue name, map reference, start time and duration. The latter is important when you are booking several shows on the same day. You will need to know how much time there is between shows so that you can get to the next show in time for the start of the performance. Be aware that most shows do not allow latecomers.

Regarding times, in nearly all cases for a particular show the start time is the same each day, but this is not true for all of them. This is particularly relevant at the Traverse Theatre, where the times and shows vary every day. Also, sometimes a particular performer, normally a comedian, has more than one show, even occasionally at different Venues. Make sure when you book that your tickets are for the right show at the right time.

The Fringe lasts three weeks but not all shows are on for the whole duration, and even those that are will have some days when they are not performing. So check carefully when planning your time that the shows that you want to see are being performed on the day you want to see them. Also, a new phenomenon in 2007 is that the same show can be performed several times on the same day, so make sure you get tickets for the right time. Monday seems to be the day when a lot of shows take a break possibly because the performers, and maybe their potential audience, are recovering from a hard weekend.

When deciding what to see, the first option is to go and see performances or artists that you are familiar with. This would normally be a comedian, a musician or a singer. For two reasons, I would not recommend this option. The first is that by visiting the Fringe you have the opportunity to see performers and performances that you would never normally get to witness and you should take it. It is also better to support the lesser known artists rather than those who could easily get an audience elsewhere.

The Fringe Half-Price Hut

The second reason is more practical. Having booked to see a few "named" shows, particularly comedians, I am normally disappointed. Whether this is due to the fact that my expectations are too high to start with I do not know. Also, if you should go to the Fringe on more than one occasion, I would advise you not to go and see the same performer a second time. In my experience, the second show is almost always an anti-climax.

So, assuming that you take this advice, you are going to need to book shows by unknown performers (at least unknown to you) and you immediately hit the basic problem: how on earth do you decide?

If anyone can provide a sure way to do this successfully, even 50% of the time, I wish they could let me know. The main problem is that individual tastes differ and one man's hilarious comedian is another's unfunny bore. Many a time I have sat stony faced through a "comedian's" performance while some people in the audience could hardly breathe for laughing. Mind you, it is normally late, they are normally students, and they are always drunk. This principle should be remembered especially when reading reviews. The person writing the review has their own personal tastes and foibles, which will not coincide with yours. They may also be biased. (More of this later).

For each entry, the Fringe programme has an outline of the show. This will be useful in giving you an idea of what the show is about, but bear in mind that it is written by the performers themselves and therefore of little value when it comes to the quality of the show. While the performer may think their show is "hilarious", it may be wise not to rely on their judgement.

An example of this occurred in 2006. The programme entry for a comedian said that the previous year, Kate Copstick had said of his show "The best show I've seen on the Fringe ... and that includes dance and theatre'. Kate is the Comedy critic for the Scotsman and she had in fact given his show a withering one star review. Apparently, performers assert that what they submit for inclusion in the programme is true and presumably there is too much information for the Fringe staff to check.

You should also be wary of shows that in the Fringe programme boast a Scotsman "Five Stars" review. Obviously it does not apply to the exact show to be put on as detailed in the programme since it hasn't happened yet. It may refer to the same show at a previous Fringe or, more likely, to a different show by the same performer or theatre group. Again, this may not be of any relevance.

In terms of the quality of a show, the only occasional use I have found for these overviews in the programme is where a show's synopsis refers to reviews of the same show at another festival, usually overseas (Canada and Australia seem to feature a lot). On the odd occasion, I have been able to find the relevant review on the Internet. In my experience, the reviews in the Sydney Morning Herald seem more reliable than those in the Metro.

So, in deciding what to see, the most useful information is going to be reviews of the current show.

Now is as good a time as any to mention the key words or phrases that you should look for, both in the programme synopsis or a review. This is of course my own list, in no particular order. With a bit of experience, you can come up with your own.

Mad Cap
Dostoevsky
Post Modern
Surreal
Unconventional
Anything with more than one exclamation mark
Must See
Freudian
Multimedia
Anything referring to an east European country
Hysterical
Physical Theatre
Anarchic
Life Affirming
Silly
Side Splitting

I would advise caution when considering any show where the synopsis in the Fringe programme contains any of the above, and if they have two or more in the same text, be it on your own head.

Newspaper Reviews

The most oft used and oft quoted Fringe reviews are those published each day (Monday to Saturday) in the Scotsman newspaper. In the past, these reviews have been more important than all the others put together, although with the Internet and other publications springing up in recent years, this is less true now. However, it is still the case that a Scotsman review can make or break a show and I assume that the Scotsman is the origin of the "Five Star Review", all their reviews giving shows from one to five stars.

For some years I have felt that the Scotsman reviews are no more reliable than any other source. Also, using my personal scoring system, I have tried to determine whether there was one or more Scotsman reviewers who were particularly in tune with my taste but I have not been able to find one. (Like all publications, the Scotsman has an army of reviewers and the name of the writer is attached to each review). I have been to see many Scotsman "Five Star" shows only to be disappointed, in some cases significantly so (see chapter 'Good, Bad and Ugly'). Likewise, I have been to see some "Three Star" shows and been very impressed. However, it is difficult to know whether the reviews are equally unreliable at the bottom end of the scale, i.e. a "One Star" show turns out to be a gem. I have not been brave enough to go and see a "One Star" show.

However, following the 2007 Fringe season, I have analysed the ratings for the shows I saw across the various review sources, both newspapers and the Internet (see "Assessing the Reviews"). I was surprised by the results.

The other national daily newspapers often carry reviews but in terms of numbers, the Scotsman prints more than the rest put together. However, they can be useful if you want to get a second opinion on a particular show. Also, it could work out expensive if you buy a selection of newspapers each day, although some reviews appear on the relevant newspaper's Web site. Be aware when looking at the Scotsman reviews that they do not include just Fringe shows. There are reviews for all the Edinburgh festivals including the International Festival and the Film Festival. If you want to see any of these performances, you cannot book them through the Fringe box Office. You will need to contact the relevant box office or Web site (see Appendix A).

In recent years, another useful source of reviews has appeared in the Metro, a free daily newspaper. Unfortunately, my own personal experience is that the reviewers in the Metro are no more in tune with my tastes than the Scotsman, and statistically they appear to be much worse (see "Assessing the Reviews").

One last point about reviews in general, it pays to look beyond the star rating. I have discovered this when checking the reviews of shows I have myself seen. Sometimes, where there is a significant difference, I have read the review and realised that the star rating does not reflect the written word, even to the extent that I feel there must be a misprint.

Internet Reviews

The other main source of reviews is the Internet. In fact, the Scotsman puts its reviews in the Web and this gives everyone the opportunity of doing some research before they get to Scotland. The Metro does the same but their reviews are more difficult to use because they do not show the star rating on the index page. You have to look at the details to determine the rating.

The List is a weekly publication and therefore their Web reviews are posted on the Internet weekly, on Thursday, rather than daily. The index page does list the ratings. Also, this publication produces reasonably up to date restaurant listings but, although there are some in each weekly edition, the complete list is in a separate publication.

One thing seems to have changed last year in that the review pages on the Internet include those for the previous year. When I first saw this on the Scotsman Web site, I thought they had made a mistake. However, I discovered that both the Metro and List sites were doing the same thing so it must be deliberate. However, it would be useful if they would allow a filter to exclude such reviews unless you particularly want them. I saw several interesting reviews for shows that had finished their run a year ago. On the other hand, when I saw that a show had returned after a "triumph" the previous year, I was able to access last year's reviews.

Note that the Scotsman's Web site includes reviews published in the Evening News and Scotland On Sunday. In fact you can often see more than one review for the same show by different critics published in different newspapers. On one level, this seems a waste. Why give one show extra publicity while completely ignoring others. On the other hand, it can sometimes be useful to get a second opinion.

Many other Web sites have sprung up and the Fringe Festival's own Web site (see 'Appendix A') has a section that enables members of the public to post their own reviews for shows. However, in my experience, these are far from reliable. It is easy to see why.

Every show has a fair number of people involved, not just the performers. It is therefore not difficult to imagine that some of the reviews on the Fringe Web site are published by interested parties. I would be particularly suspicious of any gushing review that is more than

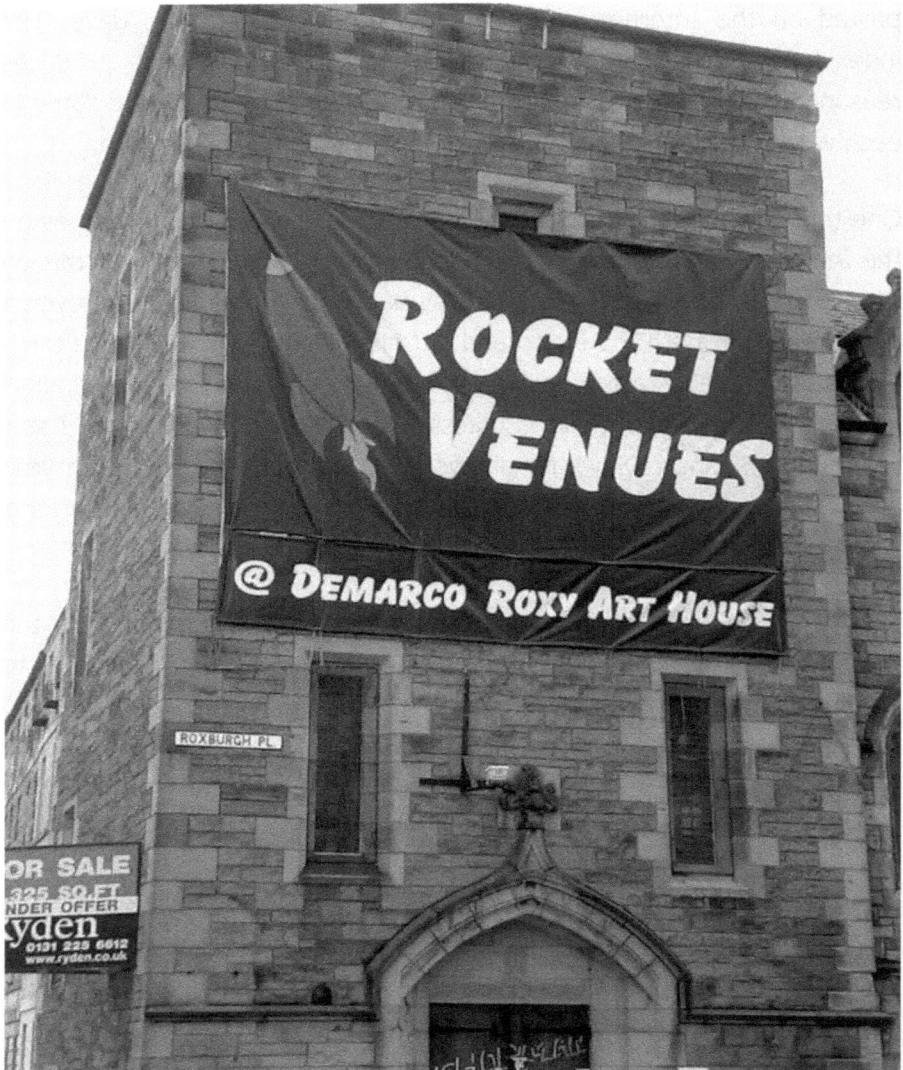
Example of a Venue using a Church Building

5 lines in length. It is probably written by someone who is sleeping with the leading man. In practice, one bad review on the Fringe Web site is worth ten good ones (unless the bad one is written by someone who used to sleep with the leading man but has recently been dumped). Another problem is that someone can give a show a good review but

forget to set the number of stars, so that they give a zero rating that in turn distorts the average score for the show. It's bizarre to think that, but for this problem, the average score for a show would be higher than the current "Four Stars".

There are now a large number of review Web sites (see 'Appendix A'), but I suspect next year some will have disappeared and more will crop up. Be careful when viewing the ratings on a Web site. In the past there was one that scored its reviews in reverse order, i.e., one star (or in this case beer glass) was a top show, five beer glasses was a stinker. I suspect that the designers of the Web site had downed a few beers when they came up with that idea.

For some of them, not only may the individual reviews be biased but the whole site may have a hidden agenda. For example, one I looked at last year, for the first week or so, concentrated on reviews from the same couple of Venues. Fair enough, not all were favourable, but the two Venues as a whole would have benefited.

The various review Web sites are updated and laid out in different ways. The most useful are those where the reviews are added chronologically. That way, if you look at a review site and then return to it a few days later, you know that all the reviews that you have not previously seen are grouped together at the start. The Scotsman, Metro and List are good for this. Since The List is only updates once a week, it can combine both a chronological and alphabetic layout. You then need a search option to find a review for a particular show.

For other sites that are arranged alphabetically it's difficult to find the more recent reviews.

One point about the review section on the Fringe Web site for a particular show is that it also refers to reviews by other publications or Web sites, i.e. The Scotsman or Metro. It does not have the star rating (some publications do not award stars) but it does have a symbol that indicates whether the review was good, bad or indifferent. Sometimes you can click on the link to go to the particular review. Frustratingly, sometimes this is not possible when you use the Fringe e-ticket tent (see Chapter 'How To Book'). There, the system restricts access solely to the Fringe Web site; otherwise it could be used as a free Internet access site.

These cross-references seem to have worked well in previous years but in 2007, they have been very hit and miss with most reviews not being mentioned for several days after it has appeared, even when it's for the Scotsman. When I used the Fringe Web site after the event to review the scores for the shows I had seen, I would estimate that more than a third of all the review cross-references were missing.

Assessing the Reviews

During the production of this book, I have considered The Fringe review process more closely than I would normally have done. The end of the Fringe season has given me the opportunity to analyze the reviews of the shows I have seen and the results are surprising, at least as far as I am concerned.

I have taken the shows I saw in 2007 and looked in the Web for as many reviews as I could find. I then compared the ratings (1-5 stars) with my own scores. For this purpose, I took an average of my score combined with that of my wife. Interestingly, on our scale of 1-10, we were within 1 point of one another for every show bar one (for some reason, my wife did not appreciate Eurobeat). For comparison purposes, our scores were changed to a scale of 1-5. I looked at two measures; how often did the scores match exactly and how often were they significantly different. By this, I mean 2 or more stars.

The results are as follows (I have included only those sites where there were 12 or more reviews of the shows we saw):

	No of Shows	Same Rating %	Big Difference %
The Scotsman	24	33	21
Metro	21	9.5	38
Three Weeks	27	26	41
The List	20	20	25
One4review	20	25	40
Broadway Baby	12	25	25
British Theatre Guide	12	42	42

These results were a something of a revelation. Whereas before the analysis, I would have thought that The Scotsman, The List and The Metro were equally useful to me in choosing shows, the statistics indicate otherwise. Of course, the figures for one year are not to taken as definitive, but the difference between The Scotsman and The Metro is striking. The figures for the British Theatre Guide bear some explanation. The difference column can be accounted for by the fact that this review site gave one star ratings to 2 shows that we rated highly.

I took the analysis one stage further and considered just comedy shows. The figures for the Scotsman were 40% same score and 20% different, an improvement on the overall score. The same exercise for the Metro gave 11% the same score and 22% different. It must be in the non-comedy area that the Metro has a significantly different opinion.

These results are obviously a personal assessment but they do indicate a basic difference between the reviews carried out by the various publications. It is just a question of finding one that suits you best. It would help if the publications gave more information about the reviewers, i.e., their sex, age and how much alcohol they had consumed before they saw the show. This is particularly relevant where the publication only exists for the duration of the Fringe. I suspect that many of the reviewers are either students or out of work actors. Personally, I will be suspicious of review publications where the writers tend to be up drinking until the early hours and sometimes miss publication deadlines. If you are the sort of person who likes to be in bed by 10pm with a cup of Horlicks, then these reviews may not be up your street.

Poster pillars outside The Assembly Rooms

Four Star Syndrome

The advent of the Internet has led to a condition that I refer to as "Four Star Syndrome". This is the situation that occurs when nearly all the shows, particularly at the main Venues, have had a four star review. This can be seen in the photograph taken outside The Assembly Rooms. Each show has a poster stuck on the pillars of the building and nearly every one of them has a banner stuck across it proclaiming "Four Stars". This is hardly surprising when there are so many review sites.

In fact, as I carried out the analysis described in the previous section, I played a game to see whether I could get a Full House for any of the shows I had seen, i.e., a show that had one, two, three, four and five star reviews. Three shows managed 4 different ratings from 1-5. (If anyone can find a 2 star review for Certified Male or Pegabovine, and three stars for Damascus, let me know). I also noticed that every one of the 32 shows bar two had a 4 star review somewhere. Furthermore, the two exceptions scored 3's and 5's.

The situation on the Fringe Web site was even more bizarre. Where the public can post their own reviews, the system displays an average rating. Of the 32 shows we saw, 29 had an average 4 star rating. Proof if any is needed that, taken as a whole, for me these reviews are useless.

Returns

In trying to find decent shows, I thought I had found a useful option. Why not go and see shows that had been at the Fringe in previous years. Surely if they have lasted a year, they must have some merit. Well it may not be a scientific survey but in 2007 we saw 2 shows in this category and they were not a success. In fact one of them was the worst show we saw that year. I should have taken my own advice and noted the reviews on the Fringe Web site (re the previous section, you can take notice of bad reviews). For the two printed reviews the average score was ½ a star.

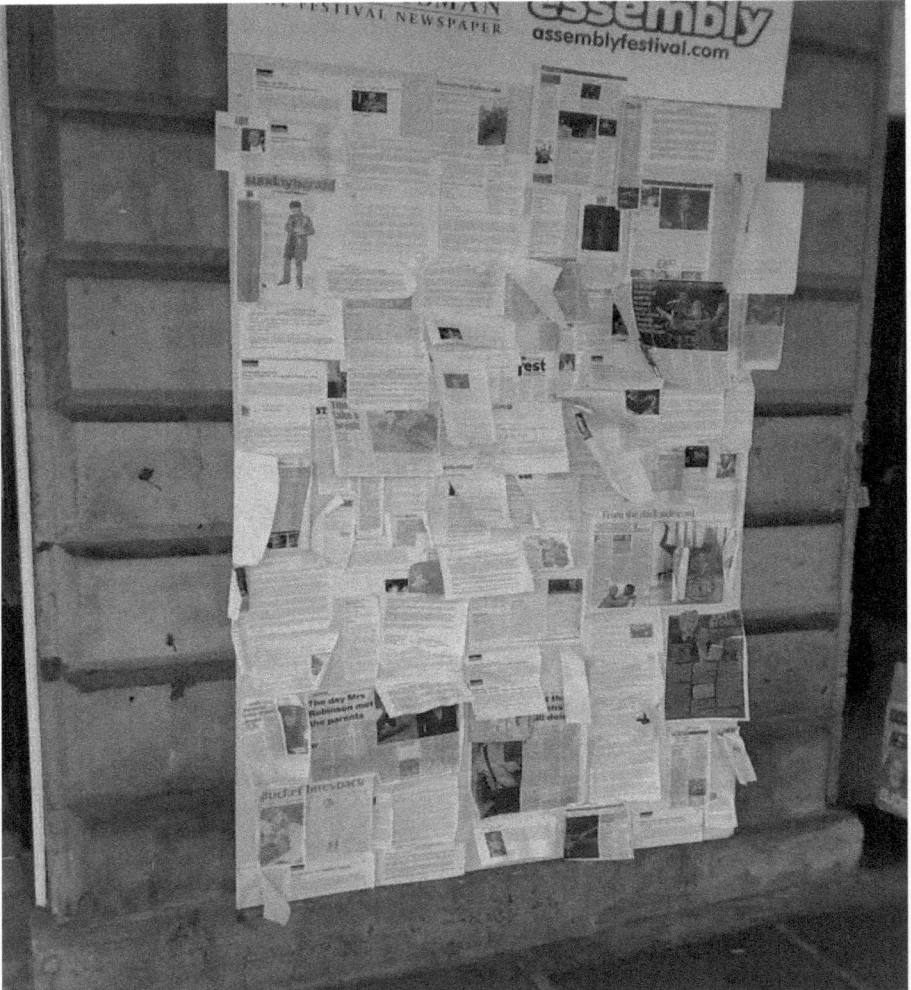
Cuttings board outside The Assembly Rooms

However, there are some shows that are a regular feature on the Fringe and they are normally worth a viewing. An example is "Puppetry of the Penis" in which two men fold their private bits into various everyday objects. The detail is displayed on a large video screen so that you do not miss anything. Ladyboys of Bangkok is another example. Here men dressed as ladies and you will spend the first 10 minutes saying how you just cannot believe it. If you are a man, you will spend the rest of the show worrying about the fact you find some of them so attractive.

Venue Postings

When assessing reviews, there is one other point to watch out for. Most Venues will post copies of reviews outside the Venue. This can be useful as it is easy to compare the various reviews for the same show. Obviously, they only post the favourable ones. However, I have spotted reviews where an extra star or two has been inked in, turning a "Two Star" show into a "Four Star" one. So I advise you to take a close look at the "stars". (In fact, as printed, the symbol representing a star is normally an asterisk, but I suppose 'Five Asterisk Show' does not quite have the ring to it).

As you can see from the photograph on the previous page, which was taken at The Assembly Rooms, the Venue reviews posted at the Venue can be haphazard. They are normally a photocopy with no enlargement so they are difficult to read unless you are very close. There is no organisation to the postings so reviews for the same show can be spread all over the board.

Stocking Fillers

Unless you go to the Fringe from day one, you will have the benefit of a number of reviews to consider before you arrive in Edinburgh. I normally make a list of the shows I want to see, where possible in chronological order of the time of day that they are performed (see Appendix D for an example). I then add to this list while I am at the Fringe as I come across things I would like to see. I find this list useful when planning my day and particularly when I need a "Stocking Filler". This is the term I use for the situation where I have a blank space in my day and I want a show to fill the gap. The main considerations are the start and end times for the show and the Venue Site. For example, if I have a show at The Gilded Balloon at one o'clock and another at The Pleasance Dome at five o'clock (they are close to one another), I may want to book something in the area that starts around 2:30 and finishes in time for the next show. My list shows me whether that is an option.

The other thing that is useful in this respect is a Daily Diary, like the one that is published in the Scotsman. This is a list of all the shows for the current day in chronological order by start time. The information for each show is brief but it will give the Venue, duration and type of show. It used to be the case that, if it had already published a review, the Scotsman printed the star rating in the Scotsman Daily Diary. However, in 2007 they only did this for the top rated 5 star shows, which made it more difficult to choose a Stocking Filler. I do not know why they did this. In previous years I thought it could be to "protect" the bad shows but since they make a point of ridiculing them in other parts of the newspaper, I doubt it. In 2007 they printed a separate list of 4 and 5 star shows but with no start times so it was pretty useless.

The Metro newspaper also produces a Daily Diary but it is not particularly useful. It does not have a Venue map, it does not include all the shows and it is broken down by type, e.g. Comedy or Theatre. Why they do this for what is basically a chronological listing is anyone's guess but it means that for finding stocking fillers, it is not as useful as the Scotsman. However, they do include the star ratings.

Some years, when they can find a sponsor, a Daily Diary is also available as a free handout. In 2007, the Guardian newspaper produced one that was included in the Scottish editions of the paper and free at various Venues and other locations around the city. It did not include star ratings nor did it have a map but in most other respects, it was the best Daily Diary. It was pocket sized and listed events from all the festivals, e.g. the Film Festival. It also included the early shows for the following day.

However, the Daily Diary is available on-line on the Scotsman's review page. Here all the star ratings are included and you have some useful search criteria.

In 2007, the best Venue map was a free one sponsored by Magners and available at the major Venues. In addition to the Fringe Venues, the map included the sites for all the other festivals including the International Festival and the Film Festival. It also included a map of bus routes in the city centre.

Awards

Another source when selecting a show are the various awards of which, in 2007, there were at least 20. The main problem is that they are normally announced towards the end of the Fringe season, so they are only of use if you are there for the last few days. For example, it used to be the case that the nominations for the Best Comedy show (Was "The Perrier" but is currently "The IF Eddies") would be announced during the middle week of the Fringe giving time to book and watch all the shows. However, a few years ago this was changed and now the nominations are announced towards the end of the third week, too late for most people.

However, as far as 2007 is concerned I need to question the quality of the nominations. By coincidence I had booked 4 out of the 5 nominees before their names were announced. They were all playing at The Pleasance and the scores we awarded them ranged from poor to average. The only one I did not see, Brendan Burns, won. However, I also saw what was generally considered to be the best comedian, Michael McIntyre, and he beat all the acts I saw hands down. It is a mystery as to why he was not nominated. It cannot be Venue bias since he was also on at The Pleasance

There is one list that is useful because it is announced at the end of each week, the Scotsman Fringe First awards for drama. They are so called because one of the criteria for qualifying is that, with a few exceptions, the first performance of the piece must be at the Fringe. Each week there are 5 or 6 nominations and in my experience, provided that you select the sort of show that will appeal to you, they are fairly reliable.

In fact, having written this I realise that perhaps I should not be so selective, having once booked a "Fringe First" show without realising that it was for children. Had I known I would not have booked it. I only found out when we arrived at the Venue. We decided to go in and see it and were rewarded with an excellent piece of entertainment. However, be warned that middle aged men who go to see children's shows without being accompanied by one or more youngsters could be viewed with suspicion. The Fringe First awards are decided by the critics on The Scotsman and published on Friday.

Talking of children, there are many shows at the Fringe aimed at children but it is possible to take a child to any show. If you are taking a child to a show that is not specifically for youngsters, check to make sure it is suitable. Shows with adult content can be shown at any time of day. The Fringe Web site does sometimes indicate whether a show is suitable for a particular age group (presumably based on information from the performers) but it is not consistent and the programme does not normally include such information.

Sample a Show

It would be easier to chose which shows to book if you could see a preview and amazingly that's what you can do.

The first option but perhaps least useful are the free performances in the street outside the Fringe Box Office on the Royal Mile. These used to be a free-for-all with acts performing anywhere on the pavement but now they are more organised on raised stages. The trouble is that the arrangement only suits certain types of show, particularly music and dance.

A much better option is the one offered by Mervyn Stutter in his "Pick of the Fringe" show. This has been running for 16 years at various Venues and Sites, most recently in the Debating Hall at The Gilded Balloon. The format of the show is that for the first 15 minutes Mervyn performs his own routine, which is a mixture of topical comedy and a couple of self penned songs. Then you are introduced to a series of short sample performances from seven or eight shows. There is a different selection each day; each performance lasts 5-10 minutes and is followed by a short chat between Mervyn and the performers. This includes information about where and when the show is being performed. The whole thing lasts an hour and a half and you can pick up flyers for the shows as you leave.

Another Church Venue

There are sometimes other shows on at the Fringe that may seem to offer a similar option but the all tend to be in the "chat show" format with singers and comedians. The Pick of the Fringe show showcases all types of performance including theatre. Indeed, the size of the performance space in the Debating Hall can allow for shows with a dozen or more performers to come on stage, do their bit, and get off in 10 minutes ready for the next act to take their place.

So this is the ideal format for such a show and if you see something you like, you can book it in the knowledge that you are going to see a good show.

Well not quite. Where I have seen a sample of a show and then booked to see the full performance, it has sometimes been the case that I have been disappointed. Unsurprisingly, the performer has chosen the best part of the show for the 10 minute segment performed on The Pick of the Fringe. I once saw a comedian who did a very funny 5 minute slot. Unfortunately, when I saw the whole show, it was the only funny bit and by then I already knew the jokes. Also, what seems very funny in front of a large Stutter audience may not be quite so amusing when there are just 10 people watching.

However, something you book as a result of seeing Pick of the Fringe is still likely to be better than anything chosen by any other method.

The Debating Hall at The Gilded Balloon is a large Venue Site and that means that during week days you should be able to get a ticket at short notice but at weekends you should book well in advance. Also, since the show is different each day, you can go more than once. It is on in the early afternoon so it is less likely to clash with other shows you may want to see.

Bear in mind that, even if you do not see something worth booking, Pick of the Fringe is worth seeing as a show in its own right.

One last option for seeing a preview of a show is the Internet. Sometimes, shows post clips of their acts on the Web. I looked at a few in 2006 but was not tempted to book any shows as a result. In fact, in certain cases, I remember being amazed that someone thought that the clip they were showing would tempt anyone to buy a ticket.

The Signpost in The Pleasance Courtyard

Word of Mouth

One of the best ways to find a decent show is to talk to other people at the Fringe. This is not as difficult as it appears.

It is often the case that you will end up sharing a table at a bar or café in a Venue. The other people at the table will normally be happy to discuss what they have seen and will probably be interested in your experiences. The same thing can happen when you are queuing for a show. Although this method is no better than most, in that different people have different tastes, it has the advantage that the views are normally unbiased (unless, that is, you are unlucky and the other person is involved in a show).

Another source of information can be the staff at the Venues. They will often get in free so towards the end of the Fringe they will have seen a lot of the shows and again they won't necessarily be biased.

Flyers

When deciding what to see, one last option is the flyers. Performers stand in the street or move around Venues handing these out to publicise their shows. In general, when it comes to deciding what to see, these are no better than the programme. However, as the Fringe progresses, if a show has received good reviews, the flyers will often have summaries stuck onto them. However, it is a good idea to check the original since the performers will have cherry picked the review references.

Previews

When reading a newspaper or an Internet site, be careful to differentiate between reviews and previews. This is particularly relevant in the first week on the Fringe. There are only so many reviewers and it takes time to get round the Fringe so the newspapers resort to publishing previews. In most cases, the pre-viewer will not have seen the show in question. There are going by previous performances by the same artist, particularly comedians, or they are using public relations material. It is best to ignore any such publicity. I do not ever remember reading a bad preview.

Partners

Having got to what I thought was the end of this section, I realise that, in deciding what to see, there is an issue that does not affect me, namely "the other person". I am lucky in that my partner at the Fringe, my wife, is happy for me to decide in general what we see and when. Provided, that is, that she has the appropriate amount of time to eat and drink. This was not always the case, but since the early years, after she made a couple of very bad choices ("Life Support" in 1991 springs to mind), she is more than happy to let me decide. We seem to have very similar tastes and she is not inclined to put in the research effort needed in order to decide which shows to book.

What people do if they do not have the same taste I am not sure. However, I have encountered several instances where we have been sharing at a table at a bar, usually The Pleasance Courtyard. The other person is someone who is waiting for their partner to come out of a show that they did not want to see. Also, at the large multi-stage Venues, there are many shows going on in parallel so rather than waiting, you can each see a different show, starting and ending at about the same time.

How To Book

There are two basic ways of booking a show; through the Fringe box office or direct with the Venue.

The Fringe box office acts as a central booking point for all the shows on the Fringe so that instead of contacting multiple box offices for different shows at various Venues, you can book them all at one place.

However, in practice this doesn't work when a show is seen to be popular. When this happens, the Venue will often withdraw all the tickets from the Fringe box office so that they can sell them direct (and so avoid paying the Fringe a commission?). Recently, for certain shows, the tickets have never been made available through the Fringe box office. So even if you contact the Fringe box office and they say they haven't any tickets, the show may not be sold out and the Venue may have some. To be fair, if you are booking by phone or in person, the Fringe box office staff will normally mention this fact.

Some of the larger Venues have their own online booking option but strangely, in 2007, The Assembly Rooms wasn't one of them. If you clicked the "book online" option on their Web site, you were taken to the Fringe Web site booking system. So, whereas for other Venues, if the Fringe box office had run out of tickets, you could check online whether the Venue had any, for The Assembly Rooms, you had to use the phone. Hopefully, in future years, this problem will be fixed.

If you want to buy tickets from the Fringe Box office, you have three choices; in person, on the Internet, or by phone. Tickets go on sale from the middle of June. It used to be possible to book tickets by post using a booking form in the back of the programme. Perhaps it is no surprise that this option seems to have disappeared.

In the past, if you wanted to buy tickets in person, you had to go to the main box office on the Royal Mile. Then a few years ago, there were a few more locations introduced. However, with the advent of the Internet, it seems that we are back to the single location, 130 High Street, on the right as you come down from the Castle. (However, see 'Half Price Hut' below). The entrance for booking tickets is down the side alley called "Old Assembly Close", which is to the left as you look at the building. If you want to collect tickets that you have pre-booked, go into the main entrance and down the stairs to the left of the shop. Note that the Fringe box office closes at 9pm so if you have tickets for collection, especially on the day of arrival, do so before this time. When you leave the Fringe box office, if you want to avoid the crowds on the Royal Mile, you can go down Old Assembly Close. It will bring you out on Cowgate. However, there are a lot of steps so I would not recommend it as a route up to the box office.

The Internet is probably the easiest way to book. The Fringe Web site allows you to book shows and the tickets can be sent to you or held for collection. In particular, when you are at the Fringe, you can use the E-Ticket Tent. This is situated on Princes Street above Waverley Station. It has 40 or more screens with access to the Fringe Web site and you can pick up the tickets at the entrance. You should try to use the screens at the far end or nearest the entrance. Those in the middle, particularly on the left, are too close to the next row and you will have people continually pushing past your chair.

The E-Ticket Tent is supposed to be used just for booking tickets on the Fringe Web site but in 2007 it was possible to book tickets directly with the Venues, useful if the show you want is sold out at the Fringe box office. To do this you select the show on the Fringe site and then click on the Venue. This takes you to the Fringe Web site's Venue page, which will normally have a link to the Venue's own Web page. Click on this and you will be taken to the Web site for the Venue. It may take some time to load so be patient. Bear in mind that in 2006 this did not work reliably but in 2007 it did. However, they may block this option in future. When you have booked your shows, make a note of the booking reference number and collect your tickets by showing your credit card at the E-Ticket box office opposite the entrance. Note that tickets booked directly with the Venue cannot be collected at the E-Ticket Tent box office.

The E-Ticket Tent

If you book tickets through the Fringe Web site, you can view your own Fringe schedule of shows booked. However, this does not include shows booked over the phone, in person or directly with Venues so is of limited value.

If you book tickets directly with a Venue, you will normally have to pick them up. They do not have a postal option.

On the subject of prices, when I first attended the Fringe, tickets were around the £2 mark. Of course, like everything, prices have gone up and the range now seems to be £6 - £10 with the larger Venues seeming to charge on average more for a ticket than the smaller Venues. So if two of you go to the Fringe and watch say 20 shows, the cost is likely to be upwards of £300. In 2007, we spent on average more than £10 on each ticket at a total cost for two of us of over £600.

However, there are ways of reducing the cost. At the start of the Fringe, for the first few days, shows often offer a "2 for 1" deal for tickets. These shows are marked in the programme. Also, if you join the "Friends of the Fringe" one of the benefits is that you can get the "2 for 1" offer for many shows throughout the period of the Fringe. The main drawback is that they must be booked in person or over the phone. They cannot be booked on the Internet. Also, the shows that offer this deal tend to be those that are expected to be less popular.

In the last few years, the Fringe organizers have introduced a Half Price Hut. As the name suggests, you can buy tickets for certain shows at half price, but only for today's performances. It is located next to the e-Ticket tent above Waverley station.

There are a few ways of see shows free of charge. As previously mentioned, the area in front of the Fringe box office enables performers to put on shows, but you will normally only get a taste of what's on offer and it is not the most comfortable way to see a performance.

The area around the National Gallery off Princes Street is usually used by Street Performers. These are often jugglers, acrobats and magicians and normally they will not be performing on the Fringe.

On the second Sunday of the Fringe a special event, "Fringe Sunday", takes place on The Meadows, which is a 10 minute walk south from the Fringe box office. It's on from 11am-5pm and features free performance of Fringe shows as well as art displays, music and children's activities. Also there is a permanent outdoor theatre in West Princes Street Gardens, which is the main open space between Princes Street and the Castle. Sometimes this has free shows but the programme varies from year to year.

But the best way to see free shows is to go to the many performances that do not charge for entry. This is an increasing feature of the Fringe and is a possible backlash to the ever increasing cost of entry to Fringe shows. In 2007, of the 2,050 shows, 304 were free to enter. Sometimes these shows are not ticketed and for others you need a ticket even though there is no charge. These can be booked through the Fringe box office in the normal way. Although these shows are free to enter, there may be some expectation of a contribution after the show but at least you can pay what you think it is worth. In deciding what to pay, if you see a good show, bear in mind what it would have cost to see the same show at The Pleasance.

Lastly, if you are at the Fringe during the last week of the festival and you want to see a show that is sold out, look out for extra shows that are added to the Fringe schedule. These will mainly be for stand-up comedians and comedy sketch shows.

Getting To The Show

Once you have taken the trouble to find a show that appeals and you have managed to book it, make sure you turn up to see it. Pretty obvious advice, but if you book 30 shows in a week, it may not be as simple as you think.

If you have booked in advance, the first thing to do each day is check all the tickets for today's shows. Check the Venues, including if you are not already familiar, the Site, the location and the start/end times. I suggest you take with you only the tickets for the current day's shows. Leave any tickets for future days in your room. If you are not yet in possession of the tickets and you need to collect them at the Fringe Office or the Venue, take with you any booking confirmation information you may have.

If you do have tickets to collect at a Venue, it may be possible to collect tickets for other Venues at the same time. The Pleasance and The Assembly Rooms have in the past shared a system, as have The Gilded Balloon and The Underbelly. If you book tickets through a Venue, you cannot pick them up from the Fringe Office, and vice versa. There was an exception to this rule in 2007. There was a problem at The Assembly Rooms and they did not have an online booking system, at least not at the start of the Fringe. Instead, users were directed to the Fringe Web site to book tickets online. If you booked tickets over the phone, you could pick them up at the Fringe box office.

TODAY'S SHOWS THE SCOTSMAN
SHOW REVIEWS DAILY IN OUR 24-PAGE FESTIVAL GUIDE

Time	Show	Time	Show
1015	PROFESSOR BUMM'S STORY MACHINE	1815	PHILL JUPITUS + ANDRE VINCENT WAITING FOR GODOT
1100	THE ONE SEA	1830	PLAYING BURTON
1100	MEN OF STEEL	1900	MAEVE HIGGINS
1100	ARNOLD WESKER'S THE MISTRESS	1930	JO CAULFIELD
1130	ALICE HOWARD AND THE MAGIC FUNERAL OF LIFE AND DEATH	1930	ADAM HILLS
1200	FORGOTTEN VOICES	1930	ROBIN INCE
1210	ROSEBUD	1940	BASIC TRAINING
1215	DICKENS UNPLUGGED	2000	CHOPPER'S HARDER THAN YOUR WAR WOUNDS
1215	FOLLOW ME	2015	NEIL DELAMERE SHOW
1215	AESOP'S FABLES — MICHAEL MORPURGO	2045	KRISTEN SCHAAL
1250	PHILL JUPITUS READS DICKENS	2055	PAM ANN
1340	A WALK IN THE PARK	2055	SARAH KENDALL
1400	LIFE IN A MARITAL INSTITUTION	2100	FRANKIE BOYLE
1400	A GLANCE AT NEW YORK	2130	LAWRENCE LEUNG LEARNS HOW TO BE AGENT...
1400	AE FOND KISS	2200	JIMMY TINGLES AMERICAN DREAM
1410	THE PITCH	2215	DAVID O'DOHERTY
1415	ROMEO & JULIET	2230	RICH HALL
1500	PRIVATE PEACEFUL	2230	THE MAGNETS
1540	JAMES CAMPBELL'S ONOMATOPOEIA	2300	VOODOO VAUDEVILLE
1540	JAMES CAMPBELL'S SPINISTRY OF MONSTERBUS	2315	INSOMNOBABBLE
1540	CALL LATE!	2354	BELLY OF THE DRUNKEN PIANO
1550	HYSTERIA	2354	BEST OF THE FEST
1600	SCARBOROUGH		
1625	RODNEY BEWES		
1700	SCARBOROUGH		
1700	MARK NADLER TSCHAIKOWSKI		
1700	AMERICAN POODLE		
1715	AN AGE OF ANGELS		
1720	TIR NAN OG		
1730	7 FINGERS — TRACES		
1800	SCARBOROUGH		
1805	BEST WESTERN BY RICH HALL		

*Show sold out. Additional tickets may be released up to 2 hours prior to the start of the performance, depending on availability

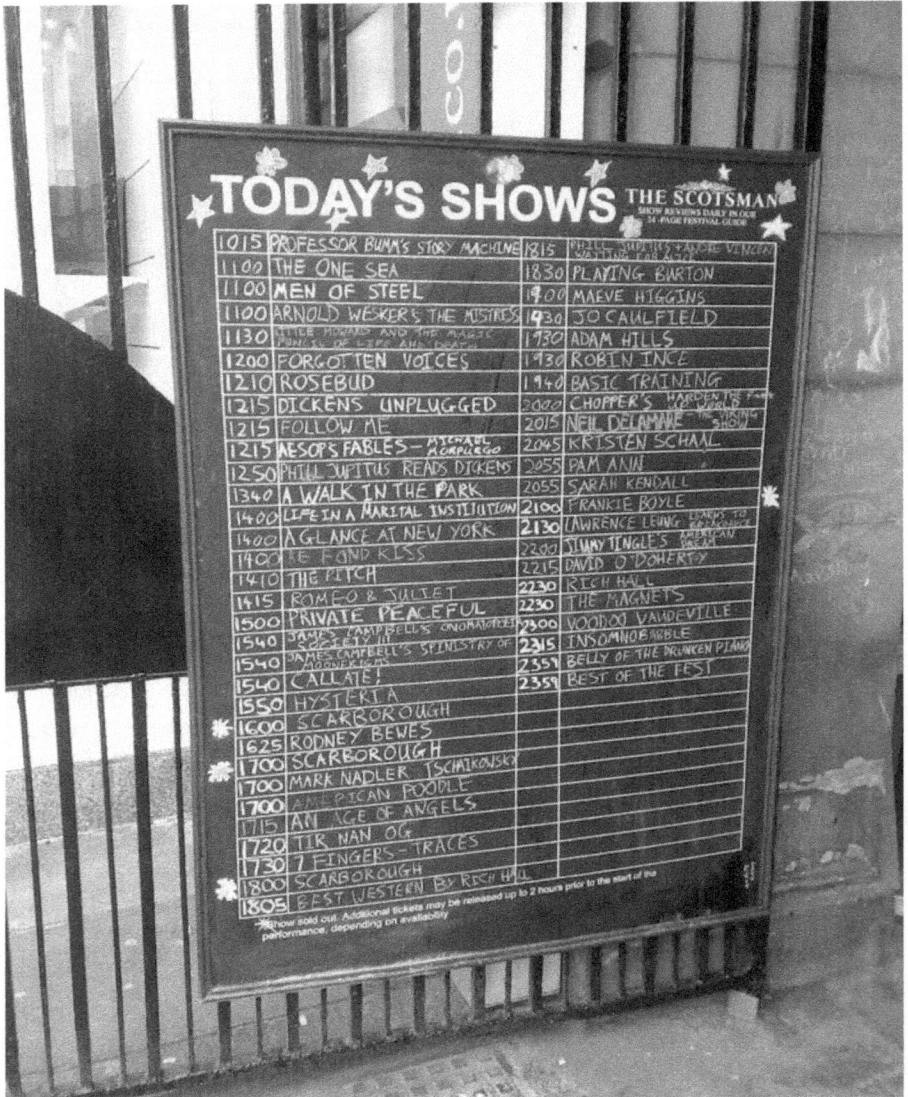

The Show Board at The Assembly Rooms

If your show is at one of the larger Venues, e.g. The Pleasance, unless you have something else to do, get to the Venue in plenty of time, especially if you need to collect tickets. You can then have something to drink or a snack at the Venue knowing that you cannot be delayed en-

90

route. For smaller Venues that do not have refreshment facilities, find the Venue first and then somewhere close by in which to drink.

The Venue Guide at the back of the Fringe Programme includes information on which Venues serve food and drink.

Keep tabs on the time and the queue for your show. If it is not particularly busy, you can probably relax until the show is called. Most shows do not have an interval so "make yourself comfortable" before you start queuing. Bear in mind that the toilet facilities at most Venues can be a bit crude. Often they are used by students for most of the year so that should give you some idea of what to expect. My wife tries to avoid using them at all but if necessary her advice in the Ladies toilets is "if in doubt, hover". She prefers to use the facilities in any of the restaurants that we frequent during the day, although she says that they are not much better.

In the early years at Venues toilet paper was a bit of a luxury, especially towards the end of the day. My wife used to take her own in her handbag. However, she informs me that in general this is no longer a common problem, although that could be because she no longer uses the toilets at a Venue.

At a busy show and at the larger Venues, the queue will start forming 10 or more minutes before the show starts. In fact, for the large stages at The Pleasance (Pleasance Grand and Pleasance One) and The Assembly Rooms (Music Hall and Ballroom), the queue will form half an hour or more before the start.

In some situations, two queues will be next to one another so make sure you are in the right one. To make sure, check with the person in front of you which show they are seeing, but bear in mind this option only works if the first person in the queue knows what they are doing. And do not assume the people checking the ticket will spot a problem, since the tickets for one show are very much like those for a different show.

Last year at The Gilded Balloon, due to bad scheduling, two shows were starting in adjacent rooms at the same time. The same ante-room was being used for people waiting for both shows. The first show was called and then we went in to our show. There was a bit of a hold up because there were not enough seats for all the audience, which is not something I have come across at a Fringe show before. Additional chairs were brought into the room and the show started. Five minutes later, we discovered the problem when 4 people in the back row announced that they were in the wrong show. They promptly got up and walked out. Neither they nor the Venue staff had checked the tickets properly.

These days, most of the tickets are of a standard design and are printed in a strip. In the bigger Venues, the tickets are checked while you are in the queue. Make sure you have them handy and keep them out after they have been initially checked, they will be checked again as you enter the room. If there is more than one of you, split the tickets up before you go in and give one to each member of your party. This will speed up the checking process and so help the Venue to keep the turn round time between shows to a minimum.

For most shows, the seating is unreserved so you can sit where you like. However, the Venue staff will often try to direct you to the front seats. Depending on the show, you may or may not want to sit at the front. For a stand-up comedy performance, you stand a good chance of being picked on. However, if you are near the front or towards the middle of the queue you will have a good choice of seats. Sometimes the seats nearest the door are reserved. This is so that latecomers can be easily admitted without disturbing the show. If you are seeing a show at one of the larger stages and you have a tight deadline to get to the next show, sit on the end of the row near the exit. However, for most shows, the number of seats is not so large as to make much of a difference where you sit.

Scoring

I am not sure how it started, but I have given my personal score to every show I have seen at the Fringe since 1991. Since this includes the first show, I can only assume that the conversation with my wife went something like:

Wife: "So what did you think of that?"

Me: "It was fine".

Not content with that vague answer, my wife pushes the point:

Wife: "Give it a mark out of 10".

Me: "Seven".

Hence my own scoring system differs from all the others that you see at the Fringe in that it is marks out of ten rather than five. This should give me more scope to differentiate between shows, but I made a fatal mistake by giving an "OK" show 7. An average show should have received 5 or 6, not 7. What this means is that I have a lot of scope to score bad shows, but not so much room when assessing the better ones. Given that over time, I have become better able to choose shows, my scoring system is little better than if I had used marks of 1-5 like everyone else. However, on looking through my scores, I was surprised to note that I have only ever awarded "10 out of 10" to two shows (see chapter 'Good Bad and Ugly').

You will not know at the start of your trip how useful it might be to record your own scores, but if you do not do so from the start, it may be too late. If you do return to the Fringe in subsequent years, it may well help you when you are selecting shows so that you achieve a better hit rate in terms of the quality, especially when trying to determine which reviews you can trust. Also, if you are with a partner or friends the scoring exercise can generate heated discussion.

The Foyer at the main "C" Venue

Over the years, I have entered all the details of the shows I have seen onto a spreadsheet. As a result, I can analyse the scores and I know that my average score each year has increased. I know that some of you will be thinking at this stage "Sad Person", but there was a practical point to this exercise. I have seen so many shows that it is difficult to remember who I have seen. Given that I do not want to see the same person more than once, this is particularly relevant with comedians. I have seen over 100 (so it says on the spreadsheet) stand-up comedians on the Fringe and if I want to book to see one I can look at the spreadsheet to find whether I have seen them before. Sometimes I see the name of a comedian advertised so often that I feel that I must have watched their show at some time but the list says otherwise.

So if you want to give the shows you see your own scores, make sure you pitch the score for the first show very carefully. It may be a good idea to wait until you have seen a few shows before you do any scoring so that you know where to pitch the average.

Eating and Drinking

I have already mentioned the fact that I am not going to give details of specific restaurants or bars in this book. There are plenty of publications that can do that. Also, if I know a good water-hole within walking distance of the main Venues and where I'm likely to get a table at eight o'clock in the evening, I am not going to do myself any favours by telling the whole wide world. (In practice, there is no such place).

The List produces a restaurant review magazine that is as good as any. You can get it at most newsagents. It includes more Edinburgh restaurants than most review books and it is probably more up to date.

If you are staying at a hotel that includes breakfast, get copies of the morning newspapers, particularly The Scotsman and Metro delivered to your room so that you can scan the reviews over the meal.

If breakfast is not included, get your papers on route to your local restaurant of choice. Note that some places that serve breakfast on weekdays are not open on Sunday mornings.

By studying the newspapers over breakfast, you will be ready to book your shows at the earliest opportunity, which is 9am for the Fringe box office and 10am for the Fringe Box Office, E-ticket Tent and the Half Price Tent.

If you do not normally have breakfast, perhaps now is the time to start. You need to build up your strength for the ordeal ahead and a hearty breakfast with a light lunch is probably better than the reverse option, i.e., light or no breakfast and big lunch. Also, you may need to be flexible with your meal times depending on the times of the shows and lunch is likely to be where you need flexibility.

The Pleasance Courtyard

When it comes to eating in the evening, you will are likely to need a longer break than you think between shows to enjoy a relaxing meal. Two and a half hours seems to be the minimum, especially if you have not reserved a table and you have to hunt for a restaurant. This is a particular problem now that many restaurants refuse to accept table reservations during the Fringe.

If you are particularly short of time you could try one of the many "eat as much as you like" Chinese restaurants that have appeared in the last few years. The main benefit is that you do not have to wait on a member of the restaurant staff to be served and the throughput of customers is so quick that, if the restaurant does not have a table when you arrive, one should be available shortly.

Of course, you could always find something to eat at one of the many fast food establishments but I find that after a busy day, where I have already seen 4 or 5 shows and there are more to come, it is good to take time to chill out over a relaxed meal.

If you are in the south east area of the city, around The Pleasance or The Gilded Balloon, the best option for restaurants are the roads that run north/south, e.g. Nicholson Street and George IV Street, and the side streets. The roads running east/west, e.g. Cowgate, Chambers Street and even The High Street are not well served with places to eat a decent evening meal.

In the area where The Assembly Rooms are situated, neither Princes Street nor George Street are good for restaurants and those that do exist can be very expensive, but the minor streets that run east/west, particularly Rose Street, and the connecting roads that run north/south, i.e. Frederick Street and Hanover Street offer plenty of choice.

Bear in mind that no matter where you are it is going to be busy. It is easier to find somewhere to eat at 6 o'clock than it is at 8 o'clock. This also helps when booking certain types of shows. In general, performances of drama tend to take place more often in the afternoon and early evening. Stand-up comedy shows take place in the evening, which the peak slot being 8-10pm. If you always eat your evening meal during this period you will be making things difficult for yourself when trying to book some of the top comedy shows. On the other hand, if you do not want to see stand-up comedy, by eating early things should work out fine.

When it comes to drinking, what you drink will be down to personal preference, but make sure you keep your fluid levels topped up. You don't want to become dehydrated. Think of yourself as a marathon runner. (If you follow my example and watch 30 or more shows in 5½ days, by the end of it you will probably feel as if you have run a marathon).

If you like beer, you may be tempted to have a pint of the local lager between shows. However, if you are watching several shows each day, these will soon mount up so pace yourself. On reflection, perhaps this is partly the cause of the condition "Ski Wednesday". Also, some Venues allow you to take drinks into the show, or even buy drinks during the performance. However, if you take a drink into a performance it will normally need to be in a plastic "glasses". Often, if you do not have the drink served in plastic, someone will be at the door to the show to offer plastic glasses to replace your glass ones.

Good, Bad and Ugly

Over the years I have seen many shows, most of which were okay at the time but, with the passing of time, not memorable. On looking through the list it is difficult to remember even one tenth of them. However, some do stick out, both good and bad, and I see no reason not to name them.

I have seen 429 shows on the Fringe in 17 years and in that time, I have only given full marks i.e. 10 out of 10, to 2 shows. These were "Cooking With Elvis" in 1999 and "Certified Male" in 2007. The latter is a good example of how you can get widely differing reviews of the same show. Kate Copstick in The Scotsman gave it 5 stars and said: "It is a joy to see theatre and its conventions so skilfully played with". However, Louise Hill on the British Theatre Guide Web site says: "I don't think I can bear to relive this particular 90 minutes in detail". She gave it half a star. Well I know which one I agree with.

Incidentally, in the same period, my wife has awarded ten 10 star reviews.

There are two shows that stand out at the bottom of the scale. The first was called "Stickmen" in 2004. This score may be a bit unfair because it was the show we saw at the Pod Venue. This was the time when we did not check the Venue location and found it had changed. After the swift taxi ride across town we were not in the best mood and the show was pretty awful. But what really grated was when, at the end of the show, one of the earnest actors made us promise not to reveal the unexpected ending to any one. Of course, had we spoken to anyone about the show it would have been to warn them off.

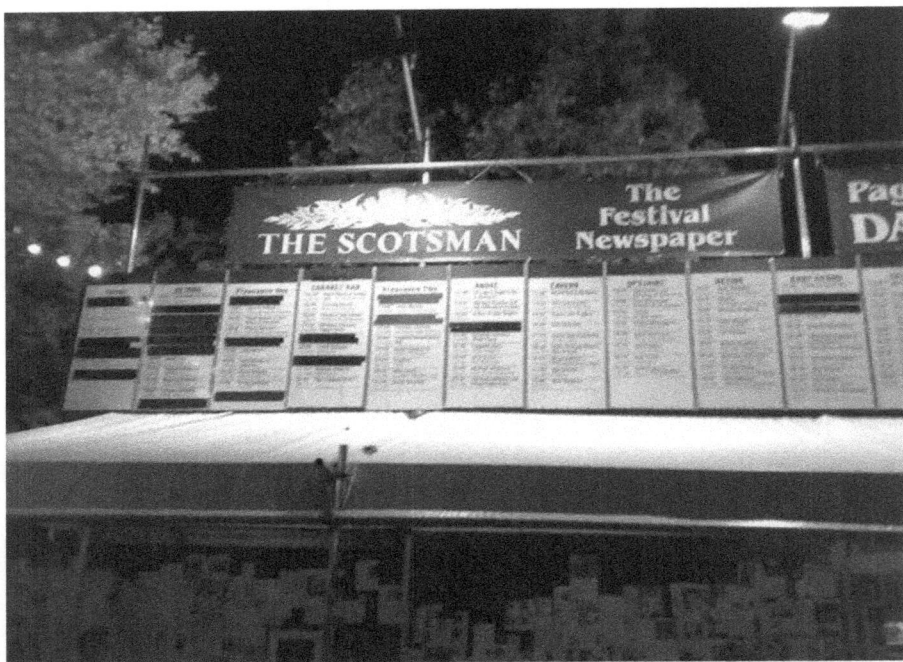

The Show Board at The Pleasance Courtyard

But the show that for various reasons is bottom of the pile (and with more than 400 shows that takes some doing) is "Noble and Silver" from 2001. It was a "Comedy" show that had received rave reviews, including if I remember rightly, 5 stars in both The Scotsman and The List. So I saved it to be the last show we saw that year. I like to try and finish on a high. We saw it in The Pleasance Above, which is one of the medium sized stages seating 150 and it was full. It was a dismal show. Unlike other forms of entertainment, with comedy it is easy to see if an audience is enjoying the show; they laugh. In this show, the entire audience sat in embarrassed silence. On reflection, I think the show was one big joke played by the performers on the audience, the climax being where for the last 15-20 minutes they played a video recording they had made of the first 15-20 minutes of the show, including the period when the audience was taking their seats.

Unfortunately, the realistic review of the show (Again, if I remember rightly, 1 star in the Evening News) came too late for us.

As for comedians, we have seen many of the top names who have gone on to fame and fortune. The scores for some of them are as follows:

1991   Frank Skinner 8 (8), Jack Dee 7 (7), Eddie Izzard 8 (8)

1992   Lily Savage 6 (5), Steve Coogan 7 (7), Jo Brand 8 (8)

1993   Donna McPhail 9 (10), Lee Evans 9 (9)

1994   Harry Hill 8 (5), Alan Davies 7 (8)

1995   Julian Clary 6 (6), Tim Vine 8 (7), Jenny Éclair 9 (8)

1996   Al Murray 8 (8), Dominic Holland 8 (8), Bill Bailey 6 (5)

1997   David Baddiel 7 (6), Graham Norton 7 (7), Jonny Vegas 9 (10)

1998   Paul Merton 6 (7)

1999   Marcus Brigstock 3 (4) Ross Noble 7 (7)

My wife's scores are in brackets.

So Donna McPhail and Jonny Vegas are the 2 best comedians we have seen on the Fringe. However, there is a good example here of the rule that you should not go and see the same act more than once. Having seen Donna McPhail at The Gilded Balloon in 1993 (The show was so funny I cannot understand why I did not give it a "10"), we went to see her again in 1994. It was just average. With comedians, they are only as good as their last joke. Indeed, even in the same Fringe season, a comedian's performance can vary greatly. Some keep to a fairly rigid script but others will play off the audience. Some do not actually get on to their planned material until half way through an hour's set. Consequently, two people can go to see the same comedian and see what is, by and large, a different show. Perhaps this partly explains differences between the reviewers' ratings.

We saw most of the comedians listed before they were famous. The exceptions are Julian Clary and Paul Merton and I think that our scores reinforce the advice given earlier in this book. If you go to see new talent you are less likely to be disappointed.

The list stops at 1999 because the comedians we have seen since that date have not yet become particularly well known. This may indicate that there is an inbuilt lead time between appearing in the Fringe and getting on the television. But it may also be due to the change in the timing of the nominations for the Fringe Comedy awards. Now that they are announced later, we do not have the chance to see them all.

Say Goodbye

Once you have finished seeing all your shows, there is not much more I can tell you about Edinburgh that is specific to the Fringe. If you are hooked and would like to return, you may want to make a note of the names of the hotels that seem suitable for you from a price and location point of view.

Open Air Theatre in Princes Gardens

One other thing to look out for is the money. Scotland prints its own bank notes but Scottish notes are not legal tender anywhere INCLUDING SCOTLAND! (I never realised this until I did the research for this book, but I have never found anyone in Edinburgh who has refused payment in either Scottish or English notes).

So you should try not to be left with any Scottish notes at the end of your trip. However, if you do have any, you can change them at a bank or try spending them in the UK. If you do try to change them, do not accept an inferior exchange rate. Also, many shops in the rest of the UK do accept Scottish notes even though they are not obliged to.

One way of getting rid of your remaining local currency would be to go to the Fringe shop, which is above the Fringe box office. You can buy mementoes of the Fringe such as tee-shirts and posters. If you plan to come again, you could register as a "Friend of the Fringe" or put your name on the mailing list for the programme.

Otherwise, that's it for another year. Physically knackered but culturally invigorated.

And just in case I get any "stick" from various quarters, perhaps I should make the following points:

The hotels in Edinburgh are all spotless. You could eat your breakfast off the floor.

The toilets in all the Venues are spotless. You could eat your lunch off the toilet seats.

The tourists in Edinburgh are all spotless. You could eat your afternoon tea off their rucksacks.

(That's enough repetition of "spotless"– ed)

The "Ladies of the Night" do not wear Doc Martins, at least not while they are on duty.

I have never met a "Lady of the Night". (That one's for my wife)

And lastly, in case anyone has the impression that "Noble and Silver" was the worst show I have ever seen on the Fringe, can I clarify the situation by saying that it was the worst show I have ever seen anywhere.

Appendix A - Web Sites

Festivals

Fringe Festival...........................www.edfringe.com
International Festival...............www.eif.co.uk
Film Festival...........................www.edfilmfest.org.uk
Book Festival...........................www.edbookfest.co.uk
Jazz Festival...........................www.edinburghjazzfestival.co.uk
Mela..www.edinburgh-mela.co.uk
Tattoo......................................www.edintattoo.co.uk
Television Festival...................www.mgeitf.co.uk

Reviews

The Scotsman - Home Page......www.scotsman.com
            - Review Page...www.edinburgh-festivals.com
The Metro - Home Page...........www.metro.co.uk
            - Review Page...www.metro.co.uk/metrolife
The List...................................www.list.co.uk
The British Theatre Guide.........www.britishtheatreguide.info
Three Weeks...........................www.threeweeks.co.uk
one4review.............................www.one4review.com
On Stage Scotland....................www.onstagescotland.co.uk
Broadway Baby........................www.broadwaybaby.com
Chortle...................................www.chortle.co.uk
What's On Stage......................www.whatsonstage.com
View From the Stalls................www.viewfromthestalls.co.uk
The Stage................................www.thestage.co.uk
Fresh Air.................................www.freshair.org.uk
FringeReview...........................www.fringereview.co.uk

Main Venues

Assembly Rooms..................... www.assemblyfestival.com
C Venues............................... www.CtheFestival.com
Gilded Balloon....................... www.gildedballoon.co.uk
Laughing Horse....................... www.freefestival.co.uk
The Pleasance.........................www.pleasance.com.uk
Rocket...................................www.rocketVenues.com
The Spiegel Garden.................www.spiegeltent.net
Sweet.................................... www.sweet.uk.net
Underbelly..............................www.underbelly.co.uk
Understairs............................www.understairs-arts.org.uk
The Zoo.................................www.zoofestival.co.uk

Appendix B – Score Sheet

SHOW NAME	TYPE	SCORE	SCORE

SHOW NAME	TYPE	SCORE	SCORE

Type = Comedy, Theatre, etc.

Appendix C – Booked Shows

TIME	DATE	DATE	DATE
11:00			
12:00			
13:00			
14:00			
15:00			
16:00			
17:00			
18:00			
19:00			
20:00			
21:00			
22:00			
23:00			
24:00			
01:00			
02:00			

TIME	DATE	DATE	DATE
11:00			
12:00			
13:00			
14:00			
15:00			
16:00			
17:00			
18:00			
19:00			
20:00			
21:00			
22:00			
23:00			
24:00			
01:00			
02:00			

Appendix D – Possible Shows

SHOW	TYPE	VENUE	START TIME	END TIME	REVIEW RATINGS	MY RATING	NOT ON

SHOW	TYPE	VENUE	START TIME	END TIME	REVIEW RATINGS	MY RATING	NOT ON

Type   e.g. Comedy, Theatre, etc.
Review Ratings   e.g. S4 (Scotsman gave it 4 stars)
My Rating   1-5 Based on reviews read.
Not On   e.g. days on which a show is not on.

www.ingramcontent.com/pod-product-compliance
Lightning Source LLC
Chambersburg PA
CBHW031520270326
41930CB00006B/457